AF599272

A BIOGRAPHY OF AMY GANNON

SUSANNA DANIEL

LITTLE CREEK PRESS®
AND BOOK DESIGN
MINERAL POINT, WISCONSIN

Little Creek Press
5341 Sunny Ridge Road
Mineral Point, WI 53565

ORDERING INFORMATION
Quantity sales. Special discounts are available on quantity purchases by corporations, associations, and others. For details, contact info@littlecreekpress.com

Orders by US trade bookstores and wholesalers.
Please contact Little Creek Press or Ingram for details.

Printed in the United States of America

Cataloging-in-Publication Data
Names: Daniel, Susanna, author
Title: Amy. A Biography of Amy Gannon
Description: Mineral Point, WI Little Creek Press, 2023
Identifiers: LCCN: 2022921427 | ISBN: 978-1-955656-41-2
Classification: Biography / Personal Memoirs

Book design by Mimi Bark and Little Creek Press

Cover photo: Mike Gannon

"Life is messy. Keep going."

—AMY

for Aaron

may you always remember the

mother who loved you so fiercely

Never stop loving your Bobbie!

CONTENTS

Madison, Wisconsin
July 27, 2022

Today would have been Amy's fiftieth birthday. I can't remember everything what we did on her other birthdays, but thanks to my photo library, I do remember some:

2006: day trip from Boston to Martha's Vineyard
2008: family trip from Boston to Maine
2010: Boston Children's Hospital for Jocelyn's broken arm the day before moving to Madison
2012: visiting London during a family trip to Europe
2014: driving down the highway to somewhere
2016: flying to Scotland for a family trip
2019: in Mazomanie to watch Jocelyn's horse-riding showcase

What's the significance of these days? In the grand scheme of life, not too much, but they represented normalcy. They represented family time. They represented spending time with loved ones. They represented life before the world as Aaron and I knew it changed forever.

There are few things worse in this life than losing your mother and thirteen-year-old sister when you are just sixteen.

It's almost impossible to explain the feeling of having your life completely changed in the matter of one evening. The day before the accident, we were having one of those family days, hanging out at the pool, playing basketball, getting ice cream, and watching Star Wars. And the day after, we were giving police our DNA to identify Amy and Jocelyn's remains.

Two and a half years later, I still don't know how Aaron and I made it through those first days. We were so fortunate to have the help of: my brother Kevin, who traveled from New Jersey the morning of the accident; Sharon Edwards of Life's Bridges, HI, who provided tremendous support and liaison with the authorities after the accident; Annie, Chris, and Haven Sadler, Kauai residents who were friends of a friend and took us into their home in the days following the accident; and the Jaye family, friends from Madison who were vacationing in Kauai at the time and also took us in during our time of need.

I'd also like to thank my life-long friends Jason Barnes and Dan Savitt who travelled back to Kauai with me to bring Amy and Jocelyn home two weeks after the accident. And several of my other friends who came to stay with us in Madison to help get back on our feet including Eli Spanier, Kevin Ormerod, Josh Tucker, and Jamie Steele. We were also so fortunate to have the support of the community when we returned to Madison. I can't put into words how much the six-month food train helped get us through our pain.

So, what positive could come out of our loss? It's hard to say there is any upside, but I thought there was one gift I could give Aaron. The opportunity to get to really know his mother.

How many people truly get to know their mothers? I know I didn't know my mother like I now know Amy. In fact, I learned many things I didn't know about her before Susanna wrote this book.

After reading through Amy's diaries, old school papers, report cards, articles, and conducting more than forty interviews with people who knew Amy throughout her life, Susanna may know Amy more than anyone.

Thanks to her, I have the opportunity to let Aaron truly know his mother. Thank you, Susanna!

Thank you to everyone reading this book to help keep Amy's memory alive.

MIKE GANNON

June 2020

Dear Aaron,

I did not know your mother. Over the months I spent researching her life, in an effort to put together a memoir for you and your future loved ones, I've come to realize that for more than a decade, I lived just a few miles from a remarkable, exceptional person—someone who I would have been thrilled to know, even in a limited way, for about a dozen reasons—without knowing it. Never meeting your mom is now one of the regrets of my life.

I've tried to understand what forces shaped Amy into the person she became, and how her signature strength, confidence, and vivacity developed from what was by all standards a difficult early life. I asked everyone who knew her how she became a feminist and an anti-racist, how she maintained her long marriage, how she found the time and energy to thrive as a mother, friend, and professional. There is no one answer, of course, but I've come to believe that the origins of her feminism and sense of justice were embedded in her early home life, during the years when her mother told her she could do anything the boys could do, while in practice showing her a way of life—depending on a man and serving him—Amy would never accept for herself. In other words, I think Amy was forced to define early what she wanted out of life, and never wavered in her determination to get it. She set her sights, and then she was off.

It's a lonely thing, though, to live a life in opposition to, or at least out of step with, the world in which you were raised. Amy's family of origin was proud of her—but could they have truly understood her life's purpose, beyond motherhood and marriage? And she made friends easily as an adult—but did those friends understand how far she'd journeyed from her childhood? Your mother was self-made in a way few people are, which takes enormous strength and confidence.

After your mom and sister died, you might have felt the adults in your life eyeing you, hoping and praying that you will be OK. They'll probably do this for a long time. I imagine there were adults in Amy's young life who looked at her the same way, with their fingers crossed for her. But no one handed her the tools to make her way—she made them for herself, and so will you.

In this book—which, it must be said, is an inadequate attempt to capture some small portion of your mother's full, foreshortened life—I've tried to highlight memories that convey Amy's core philosophies. I hope that it will be possible to one day share this book with people you love, and that they will come to know your mother at least a little, and join you and everyone who knew her in missing her, as I have.

All best,
SUSANNA DANIEL

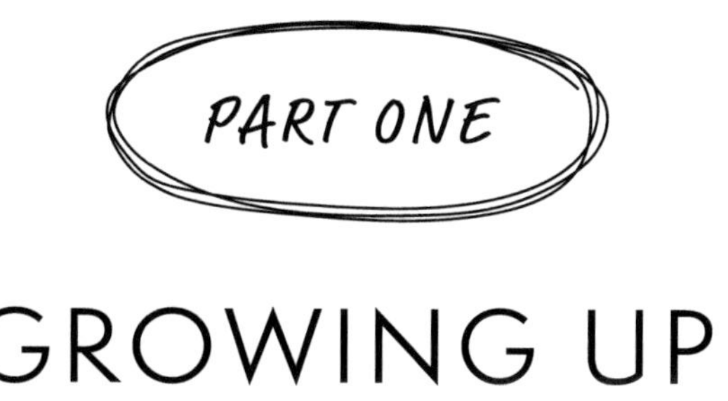

GROWING UP

"What kind of person am I? Who am I?
Where am I heading? Will I ever get to where I want to be?
Can I even be who I want to be? Who do I want to be?
The answer to all of the above questions is—
I don't know!"

—Amy, writing in her journal in 1988

June 1973

CHAPTER ONE

I wish I knew Amy's first memory, and what her childhood room looked like, and what scared or excited her when she was a little girl, what her first foods were and which ones she liked and which ones she hated. I wish I could watch a video of her playing and taking first steps and speaking her early broken sentences, and even sleeping. But I can tell you that she wore a yellow ribbon in her honey-colored, curly hair while waiting in her mother's arms for her father to disembark from his naval ship in Portsmouth, Virginia, in 1974. I can also tell you that she learned to read early, well before kindergarten, and was an easy-going toddler, capable of entertaining herself for hours.

Hope Harry met John Myers at a county fair in Ohio in 1970, and they married in 1971, when Hope was just eighteen years old. Soon after, John enlisted in the Navy in an effort to avoid the draft; his draft number was 18, which meant he would almost certainly have been called up. Amy was born on July 27, 1972, at the Norfolk Naval Hospital in Portsmouth, where John was stationed. She was just two weeks old when he sailed to Spain, Vietnam, and the Philippines on maneuvers. He was in active duty for four years, and the marriage lasted a total of five. About that time, he said, "I was home with the family less than half the time I was in the Navy. Even when I was in port, I worked twelve-hour shifts. That really hurt our marriage."

Hope remembers that time as one of struggle. Still a teenager and suddenly married with a baby, without another adult in the house, hundreds of miles from home, she had no choice but to mature early. She and John grew apart, she said, but then again, they never really got to know each other in the first place.

Doug was born three-plus years after Amy, in 1975, at the same hospital. While they were waiting for him, John took Amy to see Bambi in the theater. People didn't have VCRs yet in 1975, so this might have been her first-ever movie.

"It was just Amy and Mom for three years before I came along," said Doug. "Maybe it was easier in those days, when there were no distractions. Maybe Mom read to her back then, maybe that helped her in school. Dad got out of the Navy, and they divorced six months after I was born. Maybe Amy remembers life before our stepfather Ron came along, but I don't."

John and Hope divorced in 1976, and the next time they shared a table was forty-four years later, during the weekend of Amy and Jocelyn's memorial.

After the divorce, Hope was in dire straits. She was a remarkably beautiful young woman, just twenty-three years old, effervescent and charming, and she had a tendency to attract men who were controlling or even abusive, and to leap before she looked. So, when Amy was just four and Doug just one, Hope took them to live in Indianapolis with a man who ended up being physically abusive. What Amy remembered of this interlude in her childhood, I don't know. She would have been in kindergarten that year.

John wasn't in their lives at all during this time, so with no money and two small kids, Hope did the only thing she could do—she sold furniture to get herself and the kids back to Greenville, where she would continue to live until after Amy graduated from high school. She moved them all into the cramped and messy apartment of an acquaintance, a single woman, and a short time later met Ron Nisonger while walking home from the grocery store. Ron gave her a lift back to the apartment, where he found Amy watching TV and Doug bawling his heart out in a crib. "Get all these people out of my house," the woman said to Ron about Amy and her kids.

Ron obliged. He drove a truck and was on the road for two to three weeks at a time, so he rented an apartment where Hope and the kids stayed while he was gone, and he and Hope dated when he was in town. No doubt that many of the facts of this time are lost to history, but this is the timeline of events Doug and Amy grew up hearing about. "Maybe Amy remembered that first apartment, but I don't at all," said Doug.

Amy was five when Hope and Ron Nisonger married, after a rocky and whirlwind courtship. Once, before they were married, Hope became involved with a man living across the street and moved the kids into that man's home for a month or so. When Ron came home after a stint on the road, he took her back, and they all moved into Ron's parents' house. Next, they rented a little house on a state route in the country, and one afternoon, Doug and Amy got off the school bus, and there was no one home. Doug was in kindergarten, so Amy must have been in third grade, and somehow she knew the way to Ron's parents' house. She took Doug's hand, and together they walked the two or three miles. "It was so cold," recalled Doug. "But she made me feel safe."

When Hope married Ron, Doug and Amy were welcomed into his enormous family, which included Ron's seven brothers and sisters and his parents, who treated them just like their thirteen other grandkids.

"They were the most amazing grandparents," said Doug about Grandma and Grandpa Nisonger. "Nobody ever made us feel like anything other than blood relations." Their other grandparents, he said, never had much to do with them, so it was the Nisongers who gave them the experience of being part of an extended family.

Soon after that, Ron bought them a new house on Hog Road in Greenville. Amy and Doug each had a room, and though the house was small, it was immaculate at all times—this was something Hope insisted on. "Mom would beat us if we made a mess," said Doug. "She was crazy about cleanliness—no dirt or clutter allowed. The beds were always made as soon as we got up. She was constantly cleaning."

Hope knew how to stretch a dollar, and there was always plenty of food. Ron insisted on a big family meal when he was home, so she cut coupons and bought a quarter side of beef, canned green beans herself, made preserves from raspberries and strawberries, and at Christmas she made hard tack candy, fudge, and peanut brittle. For a time, the family filled jugs with unpasteurized milk, until that practice was ended by the health department. The kids received one gift on their birthdays and a few on Christmas, but the rest of the year there were no extras, no surprises, no unplanned spending, and Doug and Amy knew better than to ask for more. Hope had good garage sale luck, and whatever she bought at sales during one year she'd sell at a sale the next year.

"We never had any extra money," said Doug. "All of our toys were from garage sales, and most of our clothes were from thrift stores. We got about one pair of shoes every year, and maybe $100 per year to spend on school clothes."

But Doug didn't feel poor. "Ron provided for us," he said. "Life was simple. I grew up next door to grandparents I loved, we had older cars, but they worked, and we had a TV with an antenna. Going to the movies was a big deal for us—our grandmother took all the kids to see Star Wars when it first came out. I remember the lights going out and the words coming up on the screen. I'm sure Amy remembered that, too. Mom sometimes took us and a couple of cousins to the drive-in, because you paid by the carload. We'd put out lawn chairs to watch the movie."

They took one memorable vacation during the years of Amy's childhood—Ron drove them all down to Florida in his semi to visit Hope's family. In her school journal in 1984, when she was in sixth grade, Amy wrote, "Today is going great! I'm about ready to go nuts. We (my family) are leaving for Florida tomorrow morning. It's going to be so much fun. I'll get to see my grandma, Aunt Zella, another Aunt Emily, and her kids (my cousins), Ricky, and Audrey."

For the sixteen-hour drive, Amy and Doug lay head-to-toe in the bunk in Ron's trunk, while Hope rode shotgun and Ron drove. "On the way down, Amy had the chickenpox, and on the way back, I had them," said Doug.

The house where the family lived was on three acres of land, in a neighborhood with a ton of kids—most of whom were boys. Whether Amy would have been called a tomboy if all of her neighborhood friends had been girls, I'm not sure, but everyone I talked to from back then emphasized that Amy was always outside with the other kids, playing football, kickball, and baseball with them. She was the only girl in a scrum of boys.

"All summer long we played outside, and Amy played right alongside all the boys. On summer nights, we'd play until mom called us in for dinner, and after we did the dishes together, we went right back out again," said Doug.

Every year, Amy and Doug watched the Jerry Lewis telethon together on TV, both in their pajamas, and played Monopoly or chess for hours, until eventually Amy won and Doug lost his temper and threw the board; he still does this, he admitted. They sat very close to the TV and turned down the volume low and watched Friday Night Videos, which was an early version of MTV (which was an early version of YouTube, I guess?), which Amy loved. Then they did the same with Saturday Night Live. Halloween was always a very big deal in the family. Hope made the kids their costumes from thrift store stuff, with wigs and masks and props—as Amy would do decades later for her own kids—and the kids always participated in a parade down Main Street.

One hot summer afternoon, Amy and Doug and the other kids from the neighborhood begged to go to the pool, but the adults said no. The kids sneaked off anyway, and headed down the railroad tracks to the pond, where Amy stripped down to her underwear to swim just like the boys did.

"I'd always told her she could do anything the boys could do," said Hope.

Amy and Doug spent almost as much time outside during the winter as in the summer. No one in the family owned long underwear, so Hope made the kids wear last year's jeans under this year's jeans, and then the two would make tunnels and play in the snow for hours. They weren't allowed to walk into the house with snow on their clothes, so they took off everything in the back room and dashed to their rooms to get dressed again.

When she was in middle school, Amy started to make friends outside of the neighborhood, and whenever she went places with friends, Hope always made her take Doug along. "She never complained that I knew of," said Doug. "I spent a lot of time hanging out with three or four girls, doing whatever they wanted to do."

Doug doesn't remember fighting with Amy very much. They were close until their teenage years, when it started to be clear that they were headed for different kinds of lives, with her heart set on college and life beyond Ohio and his focus always on the here and now.

In 1980, when Amy was just eight years old, her father married Judy, and Amy's first half-brother Rob was born ten months later, in 1981. Cary was born fifteen months later, in 1982—they were nine and ten years younger than Amy. When Rob was born, Hope brought Amy and Doug to John and Judy's house to meet their new baby brother, and Judy remembers Amy being very excited to hold him for the first time.

The adults, however, had a tough time getting along—this was mostly John's fault, according to Hope, and mostly Hope's fault, according to Judy and John—so sibling time was hit and miss. "They told us they weren't allowed to mention their dad in the house," Judy said. If the stated rule in Hope's house was that John wasn't mentioned, the same rule was implied in John and Judy's house.

Judy was adopted and an only child, and John had twelve brothers and sisters, including a twin sister. (One died of cancer in 2007, and another was murdered by his own son in 2003, but the others live in Arcana and Greenville, with one brother in Tennessee.) John's grandmother was one of eight siblings, seven of whom became schoolteachers. Judy was fond of Amy from the start, and over the years, grew to love her fiercely. "Amy was always adaptable, confident, and easygoing," she said. "And when she was older, she tended to be blunt and always got her point across, which I respected."

Now, John regrets not pushing for more time with Amy and Doug when they were small. He diligently avoided communicating with Hope—they were oil and water, he said—and often missed his appointed time with his kids. Since the grownups didn't talk, John barely knew what was going on with Amy and Doug. He knew nothing about their sports or school lives or friends. Once, he went to the school and asked for school pictures; otherwise, he never would have seen them.

Hope remembers things from the other side—including all the times when Amy was ready and waiting for her father and he didn't show. "She would sit by the door with her coat on, waiting for him," remembered

Hope. "And most of the time, he wouldn't show up." Amy cried a lot about her father. When John didn't show, Hope would help her take off her coat, and then they'd color or read or crank up the volume on the stereo, and all three of them would dance.

"She always said I danced like a dork," said Hope—and years later, Amy would tell her that Jocelyn said more or less the same thing to Amy, like when she had worn leggings, a sweater, and boots to drive Jocelyn to gymnastics. "Grungy," Jocelyn called Amy, continuing the cycle of daughter-mother appraisal.

Once Rob and Cary were older, around ages four and five, John and Judy started to have more time with Doug and Amy under their roof. Amy loved going to John's mom's house at Christmas because there were always a lot of cousins and singing, and one of John's brothers played Santa Claus. "She liked a big party," said John. The family used to go to King's Island to see the holiday lights, ice skate, and play a lot of games. One Christmas, Judy and Amy went out and bought a new TV together so the kids could play video games. At Judy and John's, Amy and Doug didn't have their own rooms, or even their own beds, so they slept on the sofa or in the kids' rooms.

"There wasn't a lot of money, but we tried to give them all a good Christmas," said John. "Amy never complained."

Three-year old Amy
May 1975

CHAPTER TWO

• • • • • • • • • • • • • •

It's difficult to piece together what life at home was like for Amy as a young child, mostly because it's painful to recall for those few people who were also there—but there's no doubt that life with Hope and Ron was challenging, to put it mildly. Hope had an unpredictable temper and often launched fits of anger or crying without warning. Doug recalls her being inconsolably upset much of the time, often weeping under the kitchen table. Ron, who was Amy's most consistent father figure even though he was on the road much of the time, was demeaning and controlling. It's not true that Amy's childhood was an unhappy one, but it did contain a baseline level of chaos and uncertainty, where anything could happen at any time. It seems that she coped by maturing early, keeping her head down at home, and worrying about everyone else's happiness before her own.

Doug went in a different direction, often making trouble or acting out. He was a difficult and hyperactive child—these are his words—which he thinks is why Hope's erratic behavior landed more in his corner than in Amy's.

"I drove our mom nuts," he said. "She used to pull my hair back and cut it off to teach me a lesson when I was bad. Or she'd wail on me with a wooden spoon until I stopped moving. This was when I was really little, maybe from age three to ten. Amy was more mature and stayed calm, so she didn't get hit as much, though it did happen from time to time."

There's no mention of Amy being hit or hurt in her journals, which date back to 1984, when she was in sixth grade. This was the end of early childhood and the start of puberty, but there are many glimmers of the strong will and cheerful spirit she was known for throughout her childhood and into adulthood. At this point, her life was consumed by school, teachers, and friends. But unlike your average sixth grader, she was very concerned that her grades might slip—she had already decided that academic excellence was her ticket to a bigger life.

One morning early that school year (most entries are not dated), she wrote about feeling optimistic and ready for the day: "This morning my hair was looking good; my new shirt looked good with my purple pants." She complained about some teachers and praised others. "But then in Mrs. Mullin's class, I didn't have my spelling words underlined. I was mad at myself 'cause I forgot ... In Social Studies, Cary Mathis has a mild case of appendicides, [sic] and Miss Stephen started up again; she seems to think that you have it or you don't have it ... She definitely doesn't have an open mind."

Amy's best friend in elementary school was Mindy Stevens (now Mindy Libero), though that friendship wouldn't survive the transition to middle school. In April of 1986, Amy wrote that she was annoyed that her mother had made her bring a bagged lunch—but it ended up being a happy turn of events when Mindy showed up with a bagged lunch, too, and they got to sit together.

"Today is '50s day and I like it a lot. I wish we would have a dance, too, even when I probably wouldn't get asked to dance (Mindy definitely would, though)."

Throughout these early journal entries, Amy shows a healthy amount of self-awareness and levelheadedness, balanced with a touch of insecurity about boys and friends and her own appearance. In April of that school year, she wrote that she felt "kind of terrible" because two school friends, Niki and Christina, didn't seem to want her to be friends with Mindy. "Every time I try to talk to Mindy, Niki starts talking louder so I can't say anything... When I say these things to myself, it sounds like I don't want Mindy to have any other friends, like I don't want to share her, but I do and Niki has to share, too!"

In the next entry, she backpedaled. "I feel so bad about what I wrote yesterday because it's not that bad. I exaggerated and I feel mean."

At age twelve, a strong sense of compassion for others—the ability to know what you don't know—was already embedded in Amy's view of the world. In another entry, she says that she's mad at Mr. Sewell, a principal or vice principal, because he punished a kindergartner by making him sit at a table on the stage. "At that age, I feel you're just learning what's wrong and what's right during school," she wrote wisely.

In May of sixth grade, Amy signed up for chorus for the following year because, as she wrote in her journal, she liked music and she liked to sing—this would still be true forty years later. "I've always, always got the radio on," she wrote. "But I don't like Mrs. Woodbury's music class, talk about BORING! I can't stand going to her class. If we would just sing songs people like, it wouldn't so bad."

Amy dancing with her brother Doug
August 1979

CHAPTER THREE

• • • • • • • • • • • • • •

Amy's journals from her teenage years are filled with her small, precise, excessively slanted cursive, somewhere between difficult to read and impossible. In 1986, when Amy was fourteen, her mother quit smoking. "I'm really proud of her," wrote Amy. "I've promised myself I won't ever start smoking, and that is one promise I plan to keep ... It is weird but I seem to be getting a high myself because the people I love have begun to take better care of themselves, and that makes me happy."

Amy never became a smoker, but she did continue to be invested in the wellbeing of others, inside and outside of her home, sometimes to a degree that might have seemed extreme. People who knew her socially and professionally told me over and over of how when they talked with Amy, she gave them her undivided attention, as if they were her only priority, which of course was far from the case. Something about helping other people was like a source of nutrition for Amy, a fundamental part of how she got the most out of life.

When she was fourteen, Amy's journal entries started to circle around themes endemic to adolescence: boys, dating, dances, and the future possibility of sex. "No date for homecoming yet, but not stressed about it," she wrote. Then she noted that she was the only one in her class who aced the algebra test, and that she was being teased for being smart. "I used to worry people wouldn't notice," she wrote. "But I notice it, and I am proud of my grades."

When Amy was a freshman in high school and just turning fifteen, she wanted to take as many classes for college credit as possible, so she chose to take gym over the summer—but the family lived seven miles from the school, so she rode her bike every day. After class, Doug met her there, and they spent the rest of the day at the community pool and then rode their bikes home together.

It was in this gym class that she met her first official crush, Brent Yohey, who would become her boyfriend her senior year. "He made me feel special and wanted," she wrote in 1987. "I've never felt so natural around anyone else before."

But the first boy to cross a line—or almost cross a line—into romance was a boy named David, who used to go to the movies with Amy, her cousin Heather, and Hope. In August of 1987, after David left town permanently, he wrote a letter to her saying that he really liked her and had cried on the flight because they weren't going to be together.

"I don't feel the same way," she wrote in her journal. "I wrote to him and told him that my feelings weren't the same as his."

This was during the time of big hair, crimping irons, acid-wash jeans, and brand names. It was when Amy's favorite song was "Could've Been" by Tiffany (the Britney Spears of the '80s), and her celebrity crush was actor Tom Selleck (the George Clooney of the '80s). Maybe teenagers of earlier generations had to withstand the same pressure of rolling trends, but the '80s were particularly zealous when it came to fashion, music, and celebrities. "I wish I had a million dollars to spend on clothes," Amy wrote in 1987. "But I don't, so that's life."

Amy worried a lot about whether or not she would be asked out by boys. She also worried about her grades: "I've got lots of courses, and I'm afraid I'm not going to be able to keep my grade point average up!" she wrote. She wondered if she was attractive, not just to boys but to everyone. She wished when she was just turning fifteen that she had more clothes, that she were skinnier, and that her nails were longer (long nails were very important in the 1980s—there's a great photo of

Amy with freshly applied Lee Press-On Nails, which were on-trend at the time, as were her curly bangs and large, colorful earrings).

But she also wished more deeply for herself—that she were more positive, more confident, more independent of her family, that she might develop her own style, and not wear what everyone else was wearing. These are the ideas of a person who knows her mind, even at a young age.

She had hopes about the person she was itching to become. It's not rare to want to grow up faster, of course, but Amy was very specific about what being herself, grown, would look like. On August 1, 1987, she wrote, "I've been thinking about me, my life. I'm not happy with it. I want to be more. More popular! I don't care if I'm in the popular crowd. I don't want people to like me because of my friends, I want people to like me for who I am! My person, my self. I want people to have fun when they're with me. I want more people to know me and like me ...

"I'm the kind of person who wants to be the center of attention. I want everyone to like me. But nobody does, because no one wants to be a typical nobody," she wrote in August of 1987. In another entry, she wrote, "I have a lack of creativity. What's wrong with me? All I have is my grades and my fair looks. I don't really have anything that makes me stand out from others. I feel normal and average. I feel manufactured, processed. I don't really stand out. I don't mean anything to the world. Of course, I'm only fifteen. Period. Period, that's right, only fifteen. I'm feeling trapped. I can't change. It seems that no matter what, I still stay the same. I can't seem to change and make a difference in myself. I have got to work on that. I've got to change something. Soon. I'm going crazy. I'm smothering. I feel like I do what I am supposed to do according to society, well, not necessarily society but Greenville. I've got to find something I'm really interested in and pursue it."

It's difficult to imagine Amy as a typical nobody, and it's clear from talking to those who remember her from high school that even back then she left a big impression on everyone she knew. Why she didn't recognize that quality in herself, I can't say, though maybe it was something she was cultivating as she matured. Maybe standing out from the crowd didn't come as naturally as it seemed, so she worked at it until it seemed effortless. Not every teenager even wants to stand out—many prefer the opposite—but Amy was focused on her potential future self, and she showed at an early age the kind of enterprising mindset that would characterize her as a grownup. If there was something she didn't like about her life, she was going to figure out how to fix it.

Amy and her brother Doug dressing up for Halloween.
October 1982

CHAPTER FOUR

• • • • • • • • • • • • • •

Amy's first official date, the one she'd been pining for, came the night of the 1987 Homecoming dance, and her date was Tim Hurst, a senior, a football player and good student whose parents were both teachers at Greenville High. Tim and Amy met for the first time in February of that year, on a church youth group outing to see the movie "Mannequin." Amy wasn't in the church group—there was no formal religion in her home—but she went as a guest of Amy Petersteim (now Amy Floria), who was a good friend at the start of high school, though the friendship waned in later years.

Tim noticed Amy right away. "I remember flirting in the back of the van with both Amys, and I thought, 'This girl is something else,'" he said. "I loved to tease and make-up nicknames for people, and she gave it right back. She was so cute, funny, and quick. She was smart and strong willed, which I liked even back then."

Tim remembers hanging out with Amy at a pep rally, which was a typical small-town Ohio event. First, there was a parade where football players piled onto a float, and the high school band marched. It ended at the school parking lot. It was October, and Tim and Amy shared a first kiss. He was nervous when he asked her to the dance, and she said yes.

For the dance, Tim drove his dad's car and took her to Scheps Golden Lantern restaurant beforehand. He doesn't remember what they talked about over dinner, but he remembers that the conversation flowed fairly easily. The whole thing was awkward, of course, but they were both outgoing, extroverted people.

But after the dance, things with Tim ground to a halt. "He started acting like we were going to be an item, and I didn't want that. So, I told him, and he got really mad. We haven't really been speaking much," Amy wrote in her journal.

Tim got the picture. "I was way more into her than she was into me," he said. Back then, he was a seventeen-year-old boy recovering from his first brush with heartbreak—and he didn't handle it well. "I was hurt, I pouted. My mother still mentions every so often how Amy broke my heart. All these years later, I still have a crush on her. I was smitten."

What Tim was missing for Amy's taste wasn't clear, except that it seemed she had her sights more on getting to know people and dating than on locking down a relationship. "School is going great!" she wrote during her sophomore year. "I've worked at making more friends and meeting lots of new people. I am really happy because people like me!" Several boys asked her out that year, though the boys she wanted to ask her out—Jeff Marker, Pat McKinley, and Matt Caldwell—didn't, she lamented in her journal.

One boy who was special to Amy during this time was John Schipfer. She didn't record many details about their friendship, but she did write that if someone felt about her the way she felt about John, it would be "the greatest feeing."

Amy and Doug dancing to the latest cassette era hits
December 1982

CHAPTER FIVE

• • • • • • • • • • • • • •

Out of all of Amy's friends back in Ohio, the one who made the deepest impression was Shannon Edwards, who was two years ahead of Amy in school. Shannon's mother and Amy's mother were cousins and had grown up together, which made the girls second cousins.

One afternoon in 1987, when they were in tenth and twelfth grade, Amy and Shannon fixed- up their hair and shot a video of themselves dancing and singing to the song "I Wanna Dance" by Whitney Houston. Amy had big, wild hair and danced and sang with unadulterated joy—and at one point, she turned to Shannon and said that she was in the wrong skin. Inside, she told Shannon, she was a Black girl.

"People didn't talk about stuff like that in Ohio," said Shannon. "But Amy did." There was no time when Shannon knew her that Amy wasn't fiercely feminist, with a firm bent toward racial justice, though at the time, there was very little language for what interested in Amy: how to recognize the privilege of whiteness, and how to honor Black culture without being condescending or savior-minded. "There was something inside her that was accepting and open from the start, even though we were both raised in white and somewhat racist families," said Shannon.

Shannon's mother was addicted to drugs and alcohol throughout Shannon's childhood, and life at home was rough, which Amy saw firsthand. Shannon remembers Ron being more or less absent from Amy's home, and Hope being more or less unhappy. Hope once tried to open up a resale shop in the garage, with antiques and knickknacks, but it didn't succeed—which Shannon remembers being at least partly because of Ron's domineering influence.

"Her home wasn't a happy place to be," said Shannon. "She came to my house a lot, but my mom was always drunk, so we just did our own thing."

Amy and Shannon didn't party or drink. They went to the movies but didn't watch much TV, except for music videos. "We spent all of our time talking," said Shannon. "And we didn't have cooking moms, so we'd go to the park and walk, or the swinging bridge, or down to the creek to watch the water."

They never spent time or stayed over at Amy's house. Shannon remembers tension in the house, mostly directed toward Doug, who always seemed to be in some kind of trouble with Hope and Ron. In high school, Shannon dated a string of boys, including one who pushed her around. After she finally broke up with him, it was Amy who kept her from going back. "She listened to me cry and told me I was strong, that I deserved better. I know I didn't go back because of Amy," she said.

In her journal, Amy wrote that she and Shannon had seen "Dirty Dancing" together four times—and Shannon recalled seeing it with Amy a total of sixteen times (both girls worked at the movie theater). The girls bonded over their difficult relationships with their mothers and their similar upbringings.

"Neither of us had much in terms of a wardrobe," said Shannon, "but I don't remember Amy ever lamenting. We were both Kmart and layaway kids, and we spent a lot of time in thrift shops."

The next boy after Tim Hurst who caught Amy's eye was Chris Rhoades—a boy who her mother thought was cute but Shannon didn't like. "That's one reason I know I like him so much," Amy wrote in December of 1987, "because if I didn't, then it wouldn't hurt so much. Her opinion is so important. I've never had someone's opinion matter so damned much." In the same entry, she wrote that she'll only ever be just friends with Jeff and John, though she'd love to be more—especially with Jeff. And Molly was now going out with Matt, which Amy found embarrassing because she had once written him a note, presumably saying she liked him.

As with so many of Amy's negative feelings, this embarrassment seems to have had a short shelf life. She knew how to rally from a funk. "Oh well!" she wrote.

It was around this time that Amy started to feel the pull of greater independence. Her friend Amy Petersteim picked her up one night, and they drove to Pizza Hut for dinner and then to a school basketball game, which went into overtime. Greenville lost. This night gave Amy a taste of freedom she liked, and she wanted more. So, at fifteen-and-a-half, worried about her grades and procrastinating with exams around the corner, she was caught between the two worlds of childhood and growing up. Shannon, she said in her journal, still enjoyed the junior high stuff, while Amy P. was going to clubs. Then Hope gave Amy a clown box, and she asked to exchange it for a koala one. "She got me the clowns because I collect (used to) clowns. I've decided that clowns are just too young for me ... I've decided to begin collecting old photographs—antique like before the '50s. I find them interesting," wrote Amy.

Something that comes up more than a few times in Amy's journals is her concern that she hasn't had enough experience with boys. "I seem to be the only person in the tenth grade who hasn't done anything," she wrote in December of 1987.

Shannon's other best friends throughout junior high and high school were Shawn and Eric Strait, brothers and next-door neighbors, both of whom recall Amy warmly. (It was Eric who first learned Amy and Jocelyn had passed, and he told Shannon.) The foursome used to play a strip version of the card game spoons, and the girls cheated so they never had to take off their clothes.

"We would just pass the cards and make sure the other one had a spoon, and the boys sat there in their underwear, and we sat there all smug," said Shannon. "No one ever figured it out. We played hard for those spoons," said Shannon.

What Eric remembers most about Amy was his own enduring crush on her and a warm group friendship that was full of laughter. A retired school teacher named Ellen Cochran lived near Eric and Shawn, and she was known in the neighborhood as a lonely woman who would talk your ear off if you happened to knock on her door for any reason. "She would just keep talking until you said, 'Hey, I've got to go,'" said Eric. The gang—Eric, Shawn, Shannon, and Amy—thought it would be funny to record her monologues, so they did that once or twice. Once, Ellen was describing how her garage door fell on her head, and Amy said, "It came right down on you?" And Ellen said, "Honey, it didn't just come down, it KABUMPED." After that, KABUMPED became an inside joke. "We would say it to each other and giggle," said Eric.

"Eric was in love with Amy back then," said Shannon. "Everyone was." That included a French exchange student who lived with Shannon's family, whom Amy didn't like because he was a chauvinist. Shawn Strait, however, was older and handsome, and Amy had a crush on him that lasted for a long time by teenage standards. For at least a year, there was a love triangle at play, with Eric fixated on Amy, and Amy fixated on Shawn.

Amy and Eric went together to prom when he was a junior and she was a sophomore. Eric didn't have a driver's license yet, so he cooked dinner for them—shrimp cocktail and asparagus soup. She wore a light pink dress.

"She was such a happy person," said Eric. "So friendly, outgoing and goofy, and so fun to be around. Sometimes I can still hear her laugh."

Thirteen-year old Amy
June 1985

CHAPTER SIX

• • • • • • • • • • • • • •

Not having money for clothes or toys probably bothered Amy more than it bothered Doug, especially when she was an adolescent, but she never complained. In fact, in her teenage years, she made a point of talking herself out of feeling sorry for or comparing herself to other kids. In 1988, at age sixteen, she wrote, "I was just thinking of everything I have to be happy for. I have a nice house, new TV, new stereo, camcorder, telephone, a new car, my own room. I'm healthy, and my family is healthy. If I spent as much energy thinking about what I have instead of what I don't have, then I'd be the happiest person in the world. I really don't understand how my parents do it. We could qualify for government aid on our income, but we don't take it."

And she added, "One good thing about my family's income is that I'll get aid for college. That is if I'm lucky enough."

Amy knew before she was out of elementary school that she wanted to leave Greenville as soon as she could and that good grades were the way to do it. Most of her honors throughout school were academic ones—one assessment showed she needed no improvement in expressing herself in writing or in test-taking skills, which seems exceedingly accurate given who she became later in life—but back in first grade, her report card showed only one area for improvement: quiet work habits. She earned a Girl Scout Roller Skating Proficiency Award in elementary school, and in high school, she lettered in Chorus and Academics and earned a Greenville Pride Award for working on the Spanish Club Homecoming float—Spanish was one of her favorite classes, and her teacher Maxine Thomas was one of her favorite teachers —another for the Spanish Olympiad, another for "Dinner Theater Server," which likely means she worked at a school event, and another for a Paper Drive. She did not get straight As in high school—very occasionally, she earned Bs in math, science, social studies, and computer programming—and she got a cumulative 27 on her ACT. She had perfect attendance in all of 1987, sophomore year, and much of 1988.

Amy's first-ever B devastated her. This was in summer school, and according to Shannon, she freaked out and tried to get the grade changed but to no avail. This was the area where Amy was hardest on herself as a kid. Good grades might have come fairly easily to her, but she didn't take them for granted—each good grade was a step toward freedom from Greenville.

She wanted Doug to follow in her footsteps, but one of the many ways the siblings differed was in how Amy was always looking ahead, toward college and beyond, whereas Doug was happy where he was, not only in Greenville but in their home. The chaos at home didn't bother him like it did Amy; he didn't see it as something he needed to escape. When he was in high school, Amy pushed Doug to go to college, but he was never tempted.

"I'm conservative, I go to church, I'm blue collar, I'm not liberal," he said. "College pushes liberalism, and that seems like a way to divide people."

Instead, Doug encouraged his wife Kara to get her degree while the kids were still young and boasts proudly that now she makes more money than he does. "I'm not as perceptive as Amy was, not as ambitious. I focus on what I'm doing at any given time," said Doug.

But maybe he's being unfair to Amy, he said, which makes him feel guilty. "She was always kind, never insulting or condescending. She was motherly. Even as a I was growing up and raising kids, she would still mother me and tell me how to be and what to do. She meant well, but sometimes it sounded to me like she thought she knew better."

As a child, Doug assumed that Amy had left without looking back because she thought she was too good for the place where she'd grown up. "Maybe at some point that was true," he said. "But as she grew up, she softened on us."

He recalls her being his protector, guide, and cheerleader much of the time—which tells me that he knew she worried about him. In 1987, she wrote, "Doug, my dear brother, I really love him so much but he doesn't know it. Why should he? I never act very nice to him at all. I am always very critical of him and nag him about everything. I am so worried about him. His grades aren't very good, and it bothers me. I know they could be if he cared. He doesn't seem to care! He is quite intelligent I think, but he doesn't work hard enough. Why? Why doesn't he want to raise his grades? Why can't he understand how very important they are?"

As soon as she was old enough, Amy got a job. She wanted to work at the Great Darke County Fair, and eventually, she would get the chance, but first, she was hired to clear tables at the Elks Lodge. "On Friday and Saturday nights I set up, serve, and clean. It's lotsa fun," she wrote.

I'm not sure if this comment was sincere or sarcastic—but either way, the job didn't fix everything. The county fair was one of the most important social events of the year in Greenville, especially for teenagers. Locals claimed that it was the second largest county fair in the country. The whole town shut down for the week, and everyone went. Kids wore their best new school clothes, and mostly they just walked around—according to Shannon, you could play a ring-toss game for a dollar and walk away with a cane, and then you'd walk around with the cane, bumping into friends. One year, Amy and Shannon and the Strait brothers sold sodas in the grandstand so they could make five dollars to spend at the fair. In 1987, Amy wrote, "Two days into the fair and I still haven't had a date! Shit!"

Things with her mom continued to be shaky, she wrote in August of that year. "Actually, I think I've been a whiny brat and blaming everything on her. I know she loves me, but she doesn't trust me, respect me, or like me. She seems to want to run my life. I want control. I want to make my own decisions. I'm ready to grow up! I'm seriously thinking about moving into Dad's. I think he would give me more room to breathe, to make my mistakes, and learn from them."

Amy never did move to John and Judy's house, though Doug did for one year when he was in eighth grade, a time that Doug remembers clearly but Hope doesn't remember at all.

So, at age fifteen and a half, Amy was embroiled in a confusing, tenuous relationship with Shawn Strait (who would later come out of the closet, as would his brother Eric, which might explain why they were both so drawn to Amy and her free spirit and open mind) and insecure about her lack of experience with boys. On top of that, she lost her best friends. She lost Amy P. to another crowd of friends, and she lost Shannon because her psychologist told her to make new friends, according to Amy's writing. Looming over it all, Amy endured a tense home life. Hope was already aiming toward divorcing Ron—he was jealous and angry, and they fought a lot—but couldn't afford to support Doug and Amy on her own. One option was to move to Florida to be near family, but there was no guarantee of a job there.

In February of 1988, Amy wrote about the possibility of moving with her singular mix of passion, intellect, and pragmatism. "At first, I was upset about the idea. But then I figured, 'I don't really have anything to lose.' Shannon—no. Amy—no. Other friends at school—yes, but it is easy to make more of those kinds of friends. Family—no. Dad and Judy aren't really family. Grandma and the rest of them I don't really know anyway. Ron's family—that's exactly what it is, RON'S family. Eric, yes, I would lose Eric, but he would get over it," she wrote.

Amy in her prom dress.
May 1990

CHAPTER SEVEN

In March of 1988, which must have been shortly before Hope and Ron divorced, Amy's fragile infatuation with Shawn Strait got even rockier when her parents banned him from the house for reasons that are lost to history—maybe because Ron didn't like that Shawn didn't have a job at age nineteen. But Amy's response says a lot about her place in the family.

"They are always telling me I'm a snob, a miss-know-it-all. That I think I'm perfect, and that I think I'm better than everyone else. They always ask me, 'Who do you think you are?'" she wrote.

Maybe it was Amy's vision of her future outside of Greenville that made her family feel that she looked down on them, or perhaps it was her determination to go to college and see the world. To Hope and Ron, these choices must have seemed like a rejection of the lives they chose for themselves. It's likely that Hope and Ron worried, too, about Amy doing something that would negatively impact her future—specifically, that she would get pregnant and lose track of her goals.

The fact that they worried about this made Amy nuts. "Shit! Give me the credit I deserve. I'm not as damn stupid as you guys were! Fuck, what do they think, that I want to get knocked up? I go out with someone, and they think I'm going to marry the person?" she wrote.

In the spring of 1988, with Shawn mostly out of the picture and Shannon pulling away, Amy went through a period of feeling pretty low. She put on a brave face, she wrote in her journal, so people close to her didn't know she was hurting. "I'm doing a wonderful job pretending that the world is great," she wrote.

Meanwhile, the distance between Amy and her mother was growing, and Amy believed this was partly because she was building a wall between them. "I don't talk to her about anything personal, only about my future. I think it's like I want her to see me as a strong-willed, career-oriented person, only," she wrote.

As frustrated as Amy sometimes felt with her mother, she also worried about her. As a teenager, this was not her job, but there was never a time in Amy's life when she wasn't playing a more mature role in the family compared to other kids her age. She worried that Hope was a hermit—Amy's word—and that she wanted Amy to become one, too. They were close only in spurts, and they argued. "She gives me no respect whatsoever but expects me to treat her like gold. I do admit I take her for granted—often—but the road goes both ways," she wrote in August of 1987.

Hope remembers Amy being a typical teenager. "A brat," she said, laughing lightly, "and defiant." She didn't play sports in high school, just track for a while before her ankle gave out. Her room was pink and covered in posters, and the cat preferred to sleep in her room over anywhere else in the house. "She was study, study, study. She was so driven toward college. Everything came natural to her—she could read something and quote it right back. I don't know where she got that," said Hope.

Like many teenage girls, Amy felt her mother was both her fiercest ally and greatest foe. At age fifteen, she wrote, "I think I should get involved in more activities, but I feel like my mom is holding me back. If I want to do anything, the first thing mom grumps about is driving me places. It really sucks, her attitude! That's why driving is sooo important to me. Mom thinks I'm the worst kid in the entire world, but I really don't care. It's not true, and I know that!"

Amy did finally get her driver's license just before she graduated from high school, after taking classes at Neal's Driving School in May of 1990. Doug said that his mother said she tried to teach Amy to drive, but she accidentally drove into a trash can, then got out and never tried again. "But mom's stories are skewed," Doug added.

It was a tumultuous time of life, no doubt, and Amy clearly got through it. But knowing how confident and strong she became later, it's worth recalling that she made herself that way over time, and that as a young adult, she beat herself up like everyone else does.

"I look like a fool. I feel like a fool. If I try to do anything, I don't do it right. Shit!" she wrote.

It's difficult to know how much entries in an old journal can tell us about a person's whole heart and soul at any given time, since we tend to write mostly when we're feeling lost, upset, or confused. But what I think is so profound about Amy's writing from later in high school is how actively she was seeking to change her life and grow into the person she wanted to be. She was never passive or accepting of anything about her home, school, or friendships—she was always thinking of ways to improve things, including herself. Thinking this way, about how to change and grow in the right direction, is one thing that distinguished Amy from other kids and part of why everyone described her as mature for her age.

In 1988, she wrote, "I'm not happy with the person I am. I'm not even a person because I can't figure out who I am, who I want to be. I don't know what I believe, feel, like. My opinions and everything change from day to day. I am so confused! I can't figure anything or anyone. What do other people see? I don't know. I'm not doing anything. I've been so confused for so long that I've just been existing, nothing more! It's got to stop; it's got to change now.

"What kind of person am I? Who am I? Where am I heading? Will I ever get to where I want to be? Can I even be who I want to be? Who do I want to be? The answer to all of the above questions is—I don't know! Simply and I don't know how to find out.

"How does my physical self really look to everyone? What does my emotional and mental self look to everyone? To me, my mind is nothing. I don't like my personality very much. The personality I'm living now anyway. Well, actually I'm living about ten different personalities. Which is really me? Do I have to choose? I have to have one to concentrate on to direct myself towards! Who?"

Meanwhile, Amy's relationship with Ron, which had never been warm or supportive, worsened during Amy's sophomore and junior years. Among all of the ranting that she did on the page about the frustrations of teenage life—not being understood by parents, not having control of her own life—one thing that never wavers is her unceasing resentment of Ron, whom she sometimes refers to as Dad.

"Sometimes we don't talk for three weeks," she wrote, "yet he still thinks he knows me."

Doug has mostly positive or at least neutral things to say about their stepfather, but according to him and Hope, Ron was brash and insulting to Amy, remarking on her weight, her hair, and even her brains, all of which he claimed was teasing. "Mophead," he called her because of her wild, curly hair.

"He called Amy names and hurt her feelings; he emotionally and verbally abused her. It could have been much worse if our mom had married someone else and we'd been in a different situation. I feel gratitude toward Ron for the family life he brought to our home, along with the stability and safety, but I'm still sad about how it was," said Doug. "But Mom did the best she could, given her mental health."

Amy never liked Ron and didn't pretend otherwise. In February of 1988, she wrote, "Yesterday Ron came home, and almost immediately, he and Mom began arguing. It hurts so much to see Mom so unhappy. They fight a lot about me. I don't really feel guilty though. I mean, what can I do about it? I don't agree with Ron. He doesn't know me let alone love me. How can he judge me? How can he say what I think or want or feel? He doesn't know! He doesn't care about me, and I couldn't care less. I don't want him to love me or care about me or have any part in my life at all!"

It's painful to think of Amy having to live with someone she thought of this way, tiptoeing around him when he wasn't on the road, always aware that she might step into his crossfire.

Doug had very different relationship with Ron than Amy did, partly because he was younger and a boy, and partly because he needed Ron more than Amy did. "Ron was all I had in terms of a male role model," he said. "Throughout my teen years, when my mom went nuts or got angry or threw out my stuff, he was steady and solid. He helped me stay out of trouble, and he always showed up. He's one reason I became solid, myself."

Hope and Ron finally divorced when Amy was sixteen and Doug was thirteen. Ron stayed in the house, and Hope moved herself and the kids to an apartment in town, which Amy liked because it was easier to go out and meet up with friends.

After this, Amy's social life tipped further toward freedom, independence, and adulthood. She'd long held a dream of partying on New Year's Eve, and during her senior year—while dating Brent Yohey—that dream came true.

"I have had more fun on this Christmas vacation that I've ever had before. My friends and I went to the spaghetti warehouse, the Odyssey [a dance club]. Then the next day Jodi, Gretchen, Brent, and I went to Casa Lupita and the Odyssey. We had so much fun. Brent and I both had to work on New Year's Eve, but we got off at eleven o'clock and went to his house. They were a bunch of people there already. I got drunk off my ass for the first time in my life. Brent took care of me though. He didn't let me hurt myself or anyone else, and he didn't take advantage of me."

Shortly after that, she neglected to call home after going to Brent's after school, and ended up being grounded—no telephone—for two weeks.

"I think another thing about mom is that every day she realizes college is coming closer and closer, and she is afraid. She doesn't want me to go away and is trying to be Super Mom. I think she starts to feel sometimes like she's neglecting us then overcompensates. She's basically a great mom, and I love her more than she'll ever know, but she's just being stupid! This won't be the last two weeks of my life—I'll live—no use brooding over it!" wrote Amy.

When Amy was a senior in high school, she flew out to Albuquerque to visit Shannon and a boy she was living with for a week. On that trip, Amy witnessed Shannon's then-boyfriend hit her, and she told Shannon's family when she returned home.

"She was there for the worst of the worst," said Shannon.

Amy was never temperamental or dramatic when things were tough, Shannon said, though she had a face she wore when she was frustrated or angry, a face Shannon will never forget. Amy was dependable and a great listener, and she was always there for Shannon, who thinks that, looking back, the friendship was too much of a one-way street. "She took such good care of me. But I didn't know a lot about what was going on in her head. I would have listened, but she didn't share," she said.

Hope also remarked on Amy's mixture of openness and privacy. "She was so expressive, but she also kept a lot inside," she said.

Shannon isn't the only person in Amy's life who sometimes felt that Amy was more comfortable lending an ear than she was confiding in others. But being deeply known for her whole authentic self was important to Amy even as a teenager, and this comes up again and again in her journals. Shannon knew her, she said. Eric also knew her. The relationship with Shawn never got to the point where he knew her well, and that was something she regretted, and for which she blamed her parents. The last years of high school were the rockiest between Amy and Hope, and it seems like much of the time, they were each guessing at what the other was thinking.

Her senior year, Amy wrote, "Mom—we argue a lot, but I love her. We argue, argue! She can be so close minded. She doesn't really know me either. She may think she does, but she doesn't. How can she when she doesn't care about anything I think or feel? She's always ragging me about being a wife. Saying I should learn to cook and clean etc. All these so-called 'womanly' things, if I ever want to get married. Even. She's continually pressuring me. She doesn't see anything interesting in me. I don't either."

Shannon, too, said that Amy was far from sure that she would ever get married and have children. "There were so many things she wanted out of life," said Shannon. "I knew that if she did get married, it would be to a man with a huge personality, someone full of opinions and justice and life. Someone who accepted her in all forms, someone who could keep up and not need to be taken care of. She was so smart, so beautiful, so outgoing. He must have been so understanding and accepting. She would settle for nothing less."

Shannon was not at all surprised that Amy did not end up replicating the kind of family she grew up in and was so impressed by your poise and sweetness at the memorial. "I saw her in Aaron," she said. "There was no mistaking her big heart."

THE COLLEGE YEARS

"Adulthood–the ultimate body snatcher."

—Amy, writing in an essay in 1991

Amy and her college friends
Fall 1991

CHAPTER EIGHT

• • • • • • • • • • • • • •

In 1990, when Amy left Greenville for American University, her challenging teenage years were coming to an end, but her brother's were just beginning. Doug attended five different high schools and never made deep connections with friends during all of those years. With Amy out of the house, he sometimes felt abandoned. "Amy nurtured me," Doug said. "She knew our situation wasn't the best before I understood that. Our mom was crazy, and our stepfather was a narcissist, so sometimes, it felt like she was all I had." For years, Doug resented Amy for leaving, but as an adult, he came to understand that she couldn't have stayed in Greenville.

The night of Amy and Jocelyn's funeral was the first time Doug had dinner with both of his parents at the same table. "We grew up in the middle of the two of them, complaining about each other and about child support. Why would Amy want to stay?" he said.

During the summer after her high school graduation, Amy and Doug worked together at something called Fair Outs, which were traveling concessions stands that moved from fair to fair for six or eight weeks at a time. They lived on the road in campers, then worked all day in the heat for tips. They were on their feet all day, selling corn dogs in one booth and fried dough and fries in another. Amy worked just the one summer, to save money for college, but Doug continued for three more summers.

"I wish I knew when she left for college how it would go after that," he said. "It had always been Amy and me. I didn't understand that she was leaving and not coming back. We were pretty normal siblings then, as far as our relationship goes, but once she went to D.C., she was gone. I didn't realize that could happen."

Doug never visited Amy at college. Hope went once, and John went once, and by the time she graduated, Doug had enlisted in the Marine Corps (he was active for just six months, then was a reservist for several years).

Amy chose American because it was known for its international studies program, and she had her eye on working for the State Department or other overseas gig. She earned a substantive financial aid package, and I'm guessing she arrived at American with less stuff—and a smaller entourage—than other incoming freshmen. ("She was kind of a minimalist before minimalism was a thing," said her college friend Warren Leyh.) If it bothered her, there's no record of it—but I'm guessing it didn't, because once she was installed in her room with her roommate, in a hall full of kids from all over the country, she made her way as she always did: with a steadfast friendliness and confidence that drew others to her.

Amy started her first year at American assuming she and her roommate Sara would become great friends—but two months into that year, she and Sara were barely on speaking terms, and she'd formed a fast, intense friendship with another first-year student named Maureen Buckley. Amy and Maureen had met during the first days of campus life.

So instead of going home with Sara for Thanksgiving, as she'd originally planned to do, she went home with Maureen, who was from Portland, Maine.

As Maureen recalls, one day she came back to her dorm room to find a note scribbled on the white board on her door: an invitation from Amy to watch the U.S. Open in Amy's room. She'd invited everyone on the hall. Maureen wasn't a tennis fan, but she was having trouble adjusting to college life and hadn't met many people, so she went. There were already a couple of people in Amy's room, and Amy invited Maureen inside like they were old friends.

"She was like, 'Hi! How are you? Come sit down!' And so I did," said Maureen. "To me, that moment encapsulates Amy."

What evolved from that first meeting was the kind of all-encompassing friendship that develops fast in times of transition and discovery. Maureen remembers Amy as a star—her word—who was always trying new things and made college life seem effortless, despite the fact that she always held jobs. "She never seemed like she was struggling," said Maureen, who admitted that despite her own relatively privileged childhood and college experience, life didn't feel as effortless to her as it seemed to be for Amy. "She came out swinging. I had way more privilege, but she was the one who led our way."

Amy and Maureen walked all over the city and beyond over that first year—they even had a plan to walk to every Giant supermarket in and around the city, and they hung a map on the wall marking which ones they'd visited. They also walked to the monuments and day by day came to know the city on their own terms.

"We were good for each other in that we really took advantage of where we lived. We just put on our shoes and went exploring," said Maureen.

For the most part, the jobs Amy held in college were pretty good resumé fodder, and she helped Maureen get work through her contacts during their first year. Through Amy, Maureen got a work-study job with a woman who studied Latin American affairs in the International Relations department. She and Amy also babysat the woman's kids.

"Amy was such a dichotomy," said Maureen. "She was graceful and a klutz at the same time, and there was something so elegant about her intelligence. She was straight-up pretty but the way she handled herself in a way made her beautiful. And then she would stumble and fall just walking down the street," said Maureen.

During her sophomore and junior years, Amy held an internship with the U.S. Trade Representative during the time when NAFTA was being prepared, and she was able to secure an internship for Maureen, too—they spent a lot of time researching the effects of trade agreements, as well as making and delivering coffee. Their good friend Chuck also worked in the executive office of the President, though he attended George Washington, so the three of them spent a lot of time together.

It was an exciting time in Maureen's memory and another example of how she and Amy made the most of D.C. It was through this internship that Amy and Maureen—and Mike—found themselves at the White House Christmas party in 1993.

There are scant journal entries from Amy's college years, and all are from her first year, before she met Mike. Maureen is a fixture in her writing, which for the most part details their hijinks, many of which involved copious drinking, late nights at bars, and very little studying.

"Mo and I are so weird!" she wrote in her journal in 1991. "We do things together all the time, and we have so much fun. One day we took a walk, and we ended up in Bethesda, Maryland!"

Later her freshman year, she went home with a friend named Brian—whom people called Doogie because he looked so young (this reference might be lost to history, but it was widely known in Amy's generation)—and visited New York City for the first time.

At the close of a journal entry in 1991, Amy summarized all the shenanigans she hadn't detailed: "Skipping letters written, letter received; drinking games won, lost, and unable to be completed. Skipping friends visiting, movies watched, and money spent ... I am now fat, broke, and flunking my classes, but I am filled with fun, friends, and kick-ass memories!!!"

In February of 1991, during her sophomore year, Amy started to find some classwork-partying balance. She and Maureen spent the occasional night in, studying in the quiet room of the library, then watching a movie. "It feels so good to sit quietly and do work. It's also cool to sit in a room with Maureen and be productive and comfortable, and it makes me all the more sure we should live together next year. For a while when we were having problems, I wasn't sure if we could live together, but now I know that we can. We are very lucky that we didn't live together this year because I am afraid that perhaps we could not have become friends, or at least remain friends through the fights we have had. Now I feel like we will always be friends in some way."

In an essay about Raymond Carver's story Cathedral, Amy told the story of watching a blind boy named Jason play Frisbee. She compared her own lack of understanding to the character's, and called attention to the great line, "Learning never ends."

As she wrote in a writing course in college in February of 1991, "Adulthood—it is the ultimate body snatcher ... It is a time when believing is no longer a function of the heart but a process of the mind."

Here's the brief essay in its entirety:

Childhood is a time of simplicity, of innocence, a time of believing. When I was young, I believed. I believed that Saint Nick was real and it didn't seem irrational for him to live in the freezing cold of the north pole with a gang of short elfin people and a herd of flying deer. And I never questioned how his old and fat and jolly body fit through the chimney where we often found small, trapped birds.

And when I was young, I believed in the Easter bunny, who came in the night in order to deliver baskets overflowing with candy and various gifts and to hide the three dozen eggs that my family had painted the night before. And, during childhood, it never once occurred to me to ask why rabbits were interested in painted chicken eggs or either's relationship to the Easter holiday. Just as it never seemed relevant why a fairy wanted children's teeth or what she did with them when she had them.

When I was young, I believed. I believed in the fairytales in nursery rhymes. Somewhere, there was an old woman who lived in a shoe with so many children that she didn't know what in the hell to do. I believe the cow jumped over the moon and somehow, a fork ran away with a spoon. I believe in Superman and super friends and Scooby Doo too. I believe that if I stepped on a crack, I could break my mother's back and I believe the knickknack and patty whack and I always gave the dog a bone. Yet, that time of youth is gone.

The time when day is day and night is night; when everything is either all black or all white. The time when I wasn't forced to determine what was fiction and what was fact; when the difference between right and wrong was exact. The time of freedom from choice is fading. Now, adulthood is creeping up behind me, asking me to abandon the filled toy boxes and summer vacations, the innocence in blind faith. Adulthood, it is the ultimate body snatcher.

Adulthood is a time of rationalizing and reasoning, a time of responsibility. Adults seem to believe, not in what makes them feel happy, but rather what makes them feel safe. They believe not in what could be, but what is: not in what they could find but rather, and what has already been found. Adults believe in work and money in life and death and cycles of beginnings and endings. Adulthood means picking and choosing what is true and what is not. It is a time when we're leaving is no longer a function of the heart but a process of the mind.

When I attempt to determine what I believe, I find it rather difficult. I am caught somewhere between the idealism of youth and the realism of adulthood. I believe in striving for balance in my life between the innocence of the young and the wisdom of the aged. A balance between giving and taking, working and playing, loving and hating. I believe in laughing and I believe in crying. I'm leaving this combination of feeling life in my heart and knowing life in my mind. And I can say that I believe in adulthood, only while cherishing childhood.

Amy and her college friend Maureen Buckley getting ready to eat lobsters
Summer 1991

CHAPTER NINE

• • • • • • • • • • • • • •

During the summer after freshman year, Amy went home to Ohio and visited Maureen in Maine. They rode bikes on Peak's Island and went camping, and their plan to live together in the dorms came to fruition when they returned to school sophomore year. "Amy was way more self-sufficient than I was," said Maureen. "She had to be—in her home, she was the grownup."

Heather Schwoebel, who became close to Amy in college and stayed close throughout Amy and Mike's time in Boston, spent a lot of time at a bar called Irish Times during their first years of college. The piano player at the bar always launched into the same song—a song with Amy's name in the title—when Amy walked through the door.

During sophomore year, Amy went back to Ohio for Christmas and returned to school unsettled and a little depressed—it wasn't a happy visit—so for a few weeks, Maureen didn't leave her side. She even brought Amy to Alexandria to stay a weekend with her mother, who had just moved there, and then to Pittsburgh to visit Maureen's grandmother. "Amy didn't want to be alone at the dorm," said Maureen about this spell. A few weeks after they returned from Pittsburgh, Amy was back to her old self, and they continued to party and study with a little more balance.

Here are a couple of poems she wrote for a class, which offer a glimpse of what occupied Amy's thoughts during this time of life.

EXCITED

I am excited.
Not like a child on his way to Disney Land.
Or like a runner in the starting block.
Not even unbelievably excited like a lottery winner.
Excited. About life.
A kind of excitement that seems to swell up inside and feels as if you are going to explode with laughter.
I am excited about being in control of my life, and being able to make a difference.
I am excited about living today. Living right now. And making the most of every moment.
Excited. About life.

BROTHER

Dear brother,
I remember your innocent smile
Your unknowing trust
I remember
When you looked inquisitively at the world
Through soft brown eyes.
Even through
The endless, hopeless questions
Ranging from
"Why is the grass green"
To
"Why do people die"
I loved you.
Even through
The battles,
The fights,
The "I hate yous,"
I loved you

Through all
The envy,
The injustice,
The rage
Even then
I loved you.
And brother,
Now you stand before me,
Innocence and unknowing trust
Lost forever.
You are no longer
So vulnerable,
So helpless.
I see your frustration,
Confusion and
Your fear.
You suddenly seem
To be growing up.
And brother,
I love you.

—Amy Myers

One of Amy's college essays was recommended for submission to The American University Journal of International Affairs by Prof. R.B. Finn, who added: "... If you edit it." Over the course of her college experience, she wrote essays on Malcolm X, the preindustrial colonization of Africa, sexual assault, gender equality in Islamic cultures, and political correctness ("Is our traditional system something to be desired?" she wrote). In an essay titled I AM LEARNING, Amy wrote about participating in a discussion section that followed a class viewing of a filmed called "The Magnificent African Cake," which was about European colonization of Africa.

"Following the movie, I joined my group in order to participate in an in-class assessment of the film. The goal was to create a balance sheet of the costs and benefits the Africans received from the European colonization. The costs in the situation were quite obvious, while the benefits were not. In our group, that essentially came down to two white women attempting to convince two Black women that they were some actual benefits. My reaction to the situation was very strong. I tried desperately to show how the transportation systems, hospitals, and schools in mere assimilation could, in the end, be considered beneficial. Though the price paid during occupation was high, there were tangible benefits afterwards. The two Black women were immovable, not for lack of trying or mere stubbornness, but due to their personal grief. So, though they tried to contemplate my ideas, they were too emotional over the subject to be 'rational' like me. My friend and I were unable to communicate with them. The longer I kept trying, the more I began to feel as though I was defending the colonizers. It felt similar to defending Hitler from World War II to an individual of the Jewish faith. I was wrong. Though I have never been prejudiced, I felt like I was being a racist. It was a horrible feeling. These girls had a heritage, a feeling for their ancestors, that I have never felt. I watched the film and felt sympathy for the Africans who are suffering and disgust for the narrow-minded attitudes of the Europeans, but during our discussion, I felt I was insensitive and callous. For the first time in my life, I truly felt guilty for being white.

"When I walked away from this class, I felt a change. For several days afterwards, I continue to think about what happened. I've begun to question my open mindedness, which I had always prided myself on, and my basic lack of experience. (I have never traveled outside of the United States.) The situation, as well as the class in general, has made me look closer at people of another culture with strong heritage of another culture. Most importantly, as it made me look closer at myself. For probably the first time in my life, I am a minority and feel disadvantage simply due to the life into which I was born. Suddenly, being a white, middle-class American is not quite up to par. Due to my lifestyle, I like the emotion, insight, and general knowledge that my Third World or minority classmates have. This one situation caused me to open my eyes to the resources I am lucky enough to have in this class and at this university. Not only can I learn the factual information from the books and reserve readings, but I can also learn the real-life stories and emotions from those in the class. This learning experience has been a signal for me to open my heart in addition to my mind."

What stands out most in this early writing is Amy's willingness to look frankly at her own lack of experience and insight—at her own innate racism or white supremacy. It would be years before she would hitch her life's work to the goal of centering marginalized voices, but the seeds were planted early.

For this piece of writing, Amy received a B.

Amy with future brother-in-law Kevin
December 1993

CHAPTER TEN

• • • • • • • • • • • • • •

Warren Leyh, who now lives in Seattle, first met Amy and Maureen in the first-year dorms, though by the time he became the third in their little gang, the two women were a fierce twosome. "By the end of freshman year, the three of us were inseparable," said Warren.

Amy was poised and confident even during their first year, when Warren was still getting situated. Unlike Amy, who went home once or twice a year and that's about it, Warren was still going home regularly to see friends and family and took a little longer to settle in. Amy was very smart, a little clumsy, and super solid, recalls Warren.

"She was so self-assured. It wasn't until I got to know her that I realized what she'd overcome to be that way. When she shared more about her high school life and not having the same supports the rest of us had, it didn't make sense to me. She was more secure in herself. So many people came to school from privileged, wealthy backgrounds, and I thought only people like that moved through the world in a confident way. Amy was an exception. Her life was full of chaos, but she was always very grounded and centered. I was all over the place, but she gave me a feeling of solidity. She knew who she was."

Theirs was what Warren called "an early, fundamental friendship," one he would recreate many times throughout his adulthood. "Still, my favorite people remind me of Amy," he said.

Warren, who is still close with Maureen, recalls that together, the two women were stronger than the sum of their parts. They were always launching capers or challenges, and they could convince anyone of anything. "Once they convinced these guys who drove a trash truck to let them ride on the back," he said.

Warren was gay but not yet out of the closet at American. Years later, when he visited Mike and Amy in Atlanta, Amy subtly let him know that she supported him no matter what—he knew she was referring to him coming out of the closet. "She radiated nurturing," he said. "Even in college, she was working to send the world in a better direction. I'm not surprised at all that she ended up so successful and doing so much good—it makes perfect sense."

Amy graduating from American University
May 1994

CHAPTER ELEVEN

• • • • • • • • • • • • • •

In January of 1991, a few months into their freshman year, Amy and Maureen found themselves spending a lot of time with a group of transfer students—including Mike, who had transferred from Ohio University.

"I knew Amy for about a year and a half before we started dating," said Mike. They spent a lot of time together in a group and even went to see James Taylor live in concert at George Mason University together, before they were a couple.

It was the following summer, between sophomore and junior year, when Amy, Maureen, Mike, and Andrea Heckel shared a house on 39th Street, along a few others. That summer, Amy and Mike had their first official date. It was Mike's twenty-first birthday, June 4, 1992, and they walked to Georgetown for dinner, then to the Kennedy Center, where they sat outside talking for a long time, then took the bus home (neither Amy nor Mike had a car in college).

Andrea, who was Warren's good friend as well as Mike's, lived next to Mike's room in the same house. One day, Andrea noticed that Amy went into Mike's room and didn't come out. She realized they'd become a couple, right under everyone's noses. "They were always together after that," said Warren.

A couple of weeks after their first date, Mike and Amy took the train to Baltimore for an Orioles game—their first-ever baseball game together as a couple—and they stood together in the vestibule of the train on the way home, kissing and sticking their heads out into the wind. In August, they went with Mike's childhood friend Juliet and Juliet's then-boyfriend (now husband) Ed to a Redskins-Vikings game. Mike and Juliet grew up together, and Juliet, who attended George Washington, starting dating Ed at the same time that Amy and Mike started dating, so the two couples hung out together a good deal. Years later, they would reunite when Mike and Amy moved to Boston, and Ed and Juliet were already living there.

In her Story of Amy and Mike scrapbook, Amy admits to having been intimidated by Juliet when they first knew each other, but Juliet only recalls being impressed with Amy in those early days. "She was very funny and social, very strong," said Juliet.

Ed recalled that Amy was friendly and open but had an edge to her. "People underestimated her because she could be quiet and cerebral at first, observing people. She wasn't shy, but she was always observing and processing."

For Amy's 20th birthday on July 27, 1992, she and Mike celebrated with an overpriced dinner at Tony and Joe's in Georgetown, and Mike gave Amy a watch and a note that expressed his gratitude for the time they'd been spending together. That weekend, Amy, Mike, and their crew had planned to go canoeing, but the weather was bad, so instead, they rented a keg and had a party. Their friend Stephanie broke her leg at that party, and Amy spent the next couple of days with Stephanie in the emergency room and the doctor's office. "Something I will never forget!" Amy wrote.

It was a summer of growing pains for Amy, Mike, and their housemates. The house where they lived was a cockroach-infested pit—this was at least partially due to Mike's tendency toward messiness, which drove their housemate Andrea up a wall—and the bills were perpetually unpaid. Their phone was turned off, then their water, and Mike ended up paying a past-due electric bill to keep the lights on. Mike was interning at Fox News and attended the Democratic Convention in Madison Square Garden.

"I was so happy when you called me from there," Amy wrote. "I remember feeling important to you. And, I remember missing you."

Mike and Amy's first concert as a couple was on August 15, 1992. They saw U2 (the first of several times) at RFK Stadium, which closed in 2019. It rained, but that didn't slow Amy down, who remembers standing in the rain singing and a enjoying a painless trip home on a bus route figured out by Mike. The following morning, Amy flew home to Ohio in the rain, feeling awful, and missed Mike while she was away.

From Maureen's perspective, Amy and Mike's relationship cemented during the fall semester of Amy's junior year, while Maureen was abroad. When she came home, it seemed to her that Amy, who had until then been her party buddy as well as her closest confidante, had settled into adulthood.

"I was surprised at first," said Maureen, "because they were a bit of a mixed match. He was quiet, and she was out there. He had this sly laugh, deadpan and sarcastic, and he was super mellow. Everybody loved Mike. He was always in the background, and she was always in the foreground. Now I can see how their personalities complemented each other. Also, he was such a dependable person, and that was attractive to her."

Warren recalls being unsurprised at the match. "They were both a little kooky, and they both always had something they were super interested in," he said. "Amy laughed a lot, whereas Mike kind of smirked and chuckled. But they're both funny and quirky. Amy took care of Mike the way she took care of everyone—she cared for people. That's who she was."

Some of their friends called them "Zany and Mike," but whatever their differences in temperament, they shared many common interests—live music and sports, theater, politics—and a similar abundance of energy. Amy got better grades, though.

"She was pretty smart and didn't have to work super hard for her grades—but she did work," said Mike.

On September 18 of that year, Amy and Mike drove with a friend to the University of Maryland to attend a rally for then-senator Al Gore, who would be elected Vice President a few weeks later. "We got there and waited ... and waited ... and waited," wrote Amy. "It was so hot. But he finally came, and you got your story." Mike was a communications major, and he had gotten press passes for his team. He set up a camera on the media stand, then reported on the event for a class project. On the way home, the car got a flat tire, and Amy learned then and there that her new boyfriend could change a flat. "Very impressive!" she wrote.

When he recalls that night, Mike gives himself very little credit. "Changing a tire is pretty easy when you're stuck on the Beltline during rush hour and have to figure out how to get out of there," he said.

On Thanksgiving of that year, Amy and Mike visited his family in Hastings, New York; her wallet was stolen in the train station en route. Then at Christmas, she flew home to Ohio but came back early because she missed Mike. "So, I bought an ugly, brown coat and got on a train to NY," she wrote.

They went into the city for New Year's Eve. "What a night! The policeman took your Absolut. We took taxis everywhere. I made us get on the wrong train. We were locked out of your house. You broke the window with your fist. Needless to say—we spent the next day in bed!"

On January 20, 1993, Bill Clinton was sworn in as the 42nd President of the United States, and Amy and Maureen—who had recently returned from a semester abroad—stood in the cold, in the South standing area of the Capitol, to witness the ceremony, as Mike worked the event as a production assistant with CBS.

Amy and Mike continued to make the most of Washington D.C. on February 26, 1993, when they waited for hours for tickets—then in an early morning entrance line—to see President Clinton speak for the first time on international policy during AU's Centennial celebration. That month, Mike and Amy saw their friend Chuck in a play at George Washington—this was for a class paper of Amy's—and ate candy bars during intermission. Two days later, Amy celebrated their first Valentine's Day by crafting a card out of magazine letters, like a ransom note. "One of the many signs I made for you," she wrote to Mike. "I think I even whined enough that I got a rose for Valentine's Day."

A life full of domestic and international travel together was ahead, and in 1993, Amy and Mike inaugurated their budding travel partnership by first taking a ski trip—Amy's first time skiing—to White Tail, then renting a car for spring break and circling the Atlantic seaboard, from Mike's parents' house in New York to Boston. In Boston, they stayed with a friend named Josh. They drank stolen champagne while sitting backstage at the Hasty Pudding Society show with Josh, who was a stage hand, then traveled to Maureen's in Maine—where Mike tasted lobster for the first time. They then went back to New York, where they were stuck in a bad winter storm, and Amy got her first taste of snow shoveling in Mike's mom's driveway.

Just like they enjoyed concerts, ball games, and travel, Amy and Mike enjoyed going out to see live theater—they would eventually become season ticketholders of the Forward Theater in Madison—and in March of 1993, they saw the popular and provocative "Six Degrees of Separation" at the National Theatre. The space was cramped, but Amy wrote that she enjoyed the production, and the more she thought about it afterward, the more she liked it. In April, they went to a Blues Traveler concert after a day of walking from bar to bar on a Pub Crawl with "the whole gang," including Mike's friend Kevin, who came to visit. The gang was separated at the concert. "We spent the entire evening looking for Maureen and Kevin," wrote Amy. "Finally, we found Maureen asleep at her apartment, and Kevin asleep on your couch. Oh well, interesting. I'm glad we were together!" The following month, they saw "Five Guys Named Moe," a musical, and went to a minor league baseball game, and then it was May—Mike's college commencement.

A photo from that day shows your father in his cap and gown with Amy by his side, both of them looking happy and impossibly young. "I was so proud of you," she wrote. "You worked so hard to graduate on time! Yeah!" Mike's family threw a party, and Amy attended as the nervous—and hungover—girlfriend.

Amy with her mother, grandmother, and first dog Sander
October 1994

CHAPTER TWELVE

• • • • • • • • • • • • • •

Amy had specific dreams. Plans. She was going to work overseas and travel, and marriage and kids seemed, to the untrained eye, like an unlikely path, yet that path started to seem inevitable when Mike and Amy settled into the basement of the house with their dog. They played the role of Mom and Dad in a house full of partying kids.

As a teenager, Amy swore she wouldn't get married and have children; Hope said this was because of her fear of making the same choices Hope had made. This was something Amy's high school friend Shannon said, too—that if she had to guess where Amy would be just four years after graduating from high school, it wouldn't be in a committed relationship with a dog and marriage on the near horizon.

"But when Mike came along," said Hope, "that was it. She loved him so much. They were so easy with one another. They had so much respect for each other."

In 1993, still in college, Mike and Amy were building a future that included their individual aspirations alongside their mutual ones. And Amy and Maureen were no longer as close as they'd been. They didn't spend hours walking and talking together, having the kinds of intense conversations they'd thrived on during freshman and sophomore year.

Amy and Mike had visions of spending the summer after he graduated living together in a cabin and working for the national parks—they made some effort to make this dream happen, but it didn't come together. Instead, they stayed in D.C., and for Mike's twenty-second birthday on June 4, he spent the weekend with friends and family in New York—and went to see Sting in concert—and Amy stayed home making a book of coupons for him, 22 in all. Kisses and hugs were included in the booklet, of course, as well as one beer, one back or foot rub, one manicure, one picnic, one trip to the store, one load of laundry, one Chipwich, one Thai brunch, one Cactus Cantina dinner, and "One coupon to win the fight!"

Rules for usage:

- Only one per day
- Depending on financial situation of the girl
- Must be used with kindness
- Girl gets kiss

Mike had found summer work with National Disabled Sports in Rockville, Maryland—now known as Move United—and he and Amy attended the 1993 World Disabled Sailing Championships in Marblehead, Massachusetts, in late August. They stayed in the Salem State dorms, where they had to flush the toilet to get cold water to come out of the sink faucet. "The place must have been haunted!" Amy wrote. She had never seen a sailing race before. "We kept sneaking off to dinner to be by ourselves!"

On December 18 of that year, Mike and Amy—along with much of their regular gang, including Maureen, Warren, and Chuck—attended the White House Christmas Party, hosted by the President and Mrs. Clinton. "It was kind of boring, but at least we can say we did it," wrote Amy.

It's difficult to ignore how many first-ever experiences Mike and Amy shared during those first heady years of their romance. By the time the White House Christmas Party rolled around, they had already taken a huge step that surprised their friends, especially Maureen and Warren, their housemates, who were still spending much of their time partying.

They got a dog.

Sander was a golden retriever, just a seven-week-old puppy when Mike and Amy brought him home over Labor Day weekend—and he would be a treasured part of their growing family for the next fourteen years. Maureen remembers Amy being mostly in charge of training Sander, though Mike recalls being a little more ready to take on dog ownership than Amy. They named Sander for Ricky Sanders of the Redskins, of whom Mike was a longtime fan.

Sander died of old age when you were very small. At the end, when he couldn't walk well, your parents carted him outside in a wagon.

In college, Amy was one of the only kids who knew how to handle the unfamiliar, cumbersome dose of independence. Later she would thank Hope for making her clean and do dishes as a kid—efforts that resulted in her early independence and self-reliance.

"She called other kids princesses—they didn't know how to do their own laundry," said Hope. "But Amy did. She knew how to get by and keep going. 'You instilled that in me, Mom,' she said. She always refused to learn to cook when she was a kid—I didn't push her on that—but I made sure she knew how to take care of things, do what she needed to do, be responsible for her own life."

Hope knew when Amy left for college that she'd never be back, and once Hope left Ohio, she never looked back, either. She credits herself for giving Amy a big dose of her progressiveness.

"The attitude in Greenville is still back in the 1950s or '60s. There's no growth there, they never change," said Hope, who debates homophobia and racism with her friends and family and always has. "My sisters never grew. My older brother did, because he traveled with the Navy, but everyone threw a fit when I lived in Peru for seven years. It was a rich experience, and I'd never change it. But my family had a problem with me living among Brown people."

Amy's sense of justice and inequity was always in place, as far as her college friends knew. It was part of her solid sense of herself and the world. "Her self-confidence was magnetic," said Maureen. "She was so fun, so well-spoken, so spazzy. And so comfortable with herself."

One difference between Amy and your average college-age kid with a strong moral compass was that she tended to keep a cool head and not make it personal. “She had a strong sense of how things should be; it really bothered her when things weren’t just,” said Heather S. “She wasn’t easily rattled by people—she tended to be more upset by systems.”

During a time of life when young people are figuring out who they are, it seemed to her friends that Amy always knew. She was so comfortable in her own skin, they agreed, that she never worried too much about what other people were doing.

As Warren put it, “Amy accepted people the way they were. She put her energy into being and becoming who she wanted to be.”

PART THREE

STARTING OUT TOGETHER

"We became ourselves together."

—Mike

Amy with our first dogs Sander and Berkeley
October 1998

CHAPTER THIRTEEN

• • • • • • • • • • • • • •

Given that your parents met and fell in love during college, every adult decision they made in life, they made together. As your father put it, there was short period after their first date on his 21st birthday when they weren't yet officially coupled—in fact, there was a night when they were supposed to meet up with Mike's cousin at a bar in Georgetown, but Amy went out with friends instead, including a friend's brother who'd caught her eye.

"I was not happy that night," said Mike. "But within a few weeks, we were pretty solid, and that was that. Neither of us dated anyone else after that."

They were still kids in many ways, but unlike most of their friends from college, Mike and Amy had made one crucial decision about the future: They were going to be together, period.

"We lived together from my senior year until the accident," said Mike. "We didn't know anything else. We learned everything together. We became ourselves together."

In September of 1994, after Amy graduated from American, they moved from Washington to Atlanta with a friend of Mike's named Dave Zorn. "Whether it was the right or wrong decision is hard to say. Maybe we could have been more successful in Washington, but we wanted to try something new," Mike said about the move. "We didn't really know what we were doing. We were going on instinct."

Mike had worked with disabled athletes for a summer, so he had some leads on a job with the 1996 Paralympic organizing committee. A month before the move, they drove down and found an apartment in the basement of a house on a hill, with plenty of windows and light and a backyard for Sander. But by the time they returned, the apartment had flooded and sustained significant damage to the floors and walls. "It was unbearably hot," said Mike about the disastrous moving day. As soon as they stepped out of the truck, they were swarmed by mosquitoes.

"Mosquitoes loved Amy," said Mike.

They were rescued by a young couple who rented the upstairs apartment, who let them stay while they searched for a new apartment. They didn't know anything about Atlanta yet, but they ended up with a pretty nice two-bedroom apartment in a building with three other units, near Emory and Virginia Highlands, and they lived there for two years. (The building has since been torn down—Mike drove by during a business trip to Atlanta in 2015.)

After two years in Atlanta, they moved to a two-flat, where they stayed for about for eighteen months. Then they moved to what Mike called "a disgusting shithole with rats," because it was cheaper.

From the start, your parents' relationship was one of equality. They were equally ambitious, equally eager to travel and work and be independent. They were more or less equally broke. In college, Amy had earned scholarships, taken out loans, and worked jobs continuously (decades later, they would disagree about paying fully for college for you and Jocelyn, because Amy believed that supporting oneself is an important part of growing up). Mike had a lot more parental support in college, though he also held jobs—but in Atlanta, they barely got by.

When they first arrived, Mike delivered food—they shared a Mazda 323 that had no air conditioning—and Amy got a temp job at the Coca-Cola headquarters. They'd been sleeping on a futon since college, and one day, they went to buy a $300 mattress, but they couldn't pay for it all at once and had to finance it over the next six months.

"We barely got by," said Mike. "Once, I remember, Amy had to choose between getting the bus home and buying herself a Coke," he told me. "I want Aaron to understand that we started with very little other than our college diplomas."

But they had each other. Once they moved from the apartment they shared with Dave Zorn, they were living alone together for the first time, along with Sander and Berkeley, their second dog, that joined them when they were living in their second house in Atlanta. Back in college, Mike's decorating style had leaned toward beer and classic rock posters, but in Atlanta, they decorated in a more grownup way.

"It was so adult," said Warren. "I remember thinking, wow, they are really happy. They were both so funny and quirky. Amy took care of Mike. Not in a pushy way, just in the same, caring way she took care of everyone. She was so solid."

During this time, Mike kept a collection of stones he'd found in lakes, rivers, and the ocean—but they were only pretty when they were submerged in water. "So, he kept them in water in containers, but Amy made him clean them and change the water every so often so it wouldn't stink," said Warren.

After the food-delivery gig, Mike started doing freelance television production work, then nabbed an internship with the Atlanta Olympics organizing committee. From there, he jumped to an internship at CNN, which segued into a full-time job in 1995.

Amy's job at Coke also opened doors for her—but she didn't want to rise in the ranks at Coke because, as Mike put it, "She didn't want to sell sugar water to people in developing countries who couldn't afford it." They were living paycheck-to-paycheck at the time, though, and Mike wanted her to take the job so they could breathe easier. She said no. She wasn't ready for the MBA yet, but she knew she could find a job that better matched her values.

Instead, she took an administrative position at the Boys and Girls Club, where she worked for a guy named Bill Kearney, who became a mentor. "They kept in touch," said Mike. "He had a lot of influence over her; he was good boss." (I was not able to make contact with Bill Kearney; the breadcrumbs I found online ran out in 2017, and the website and email addresses I found are all defunct.)

After the Boys and Girls Club, Amy went to work full-time at a Rape Crisis Center in Grady Hospital, where she became close friends with Lisa Nicholas and Rachel Van Valkenburg, who are still in touch. This was 1997.

"You could tell right away that she was smart, easy to talk to. It wasn't the easiest job, advocating for victims, but she had purpose, and she knew why she wanted to be there. And she was a goofball. And she always talked with her hands," said Lisa.

Rachel interviewed Amy for her job—she had a sense for who would work well there and knew Amy was a good fit right away—and recalls that Amy didn't match the usual profile for an employee. She didn't have a counseling background, but she had a firm analysis of violence against women. "She was wicked smart," said Rachel, "and she really got violence and misogyny and all of it. She had a really strong understanding of social constructs." Rachel was continuously impressed by her.

At the Rape Crisis Center, Amy earned a reputation early on for being willing to kick up a little dust. "Her convictions were so solid," said Lisa. "She would call people out when she thought they were out of line. She was courageous." At the time, their supervisor was a leading therapist in the field but made racist, homophobic, and belittling comments at work, and Amy went to Human Resources to report her, which resulted in the supervisor's dismissal. "She was so gutsy to take that on," said Rachel. One problem Amy reported was the supervisor's treatment of an older Black colleague named Florence, with whom Amy grew tight. For Amy, there would never have been any question that someone should be confronted for being racist or homophobic, in the workplace or out of it.

"She was a badass before that was a thing," said Rachel.

Lisa and Rachel visited Mike and Amy at home, which, at that point, was a 1950's style cottage that they'd decorated cutely. They went to see "The Blair Witch Project" in the theater and ate Thai food together. Mike was super funny, said Lisa, but dry-humored. "I figured she was initially attracted to him because he made her laugh. Amy was a great laugher. And he adored her. They were so respectful and supportive of each other." Amy never nagged or made fun of or ever said a word against Mike. "I remember knowing if I was being negative about my husband; Amy didn't play that way."

Rachel met you when you were a baby and a toddler and remembers being wowed by Amy's devotion to motherhood and marriage. "I could tell that Mike and Aaron were well and truly loved," she said.

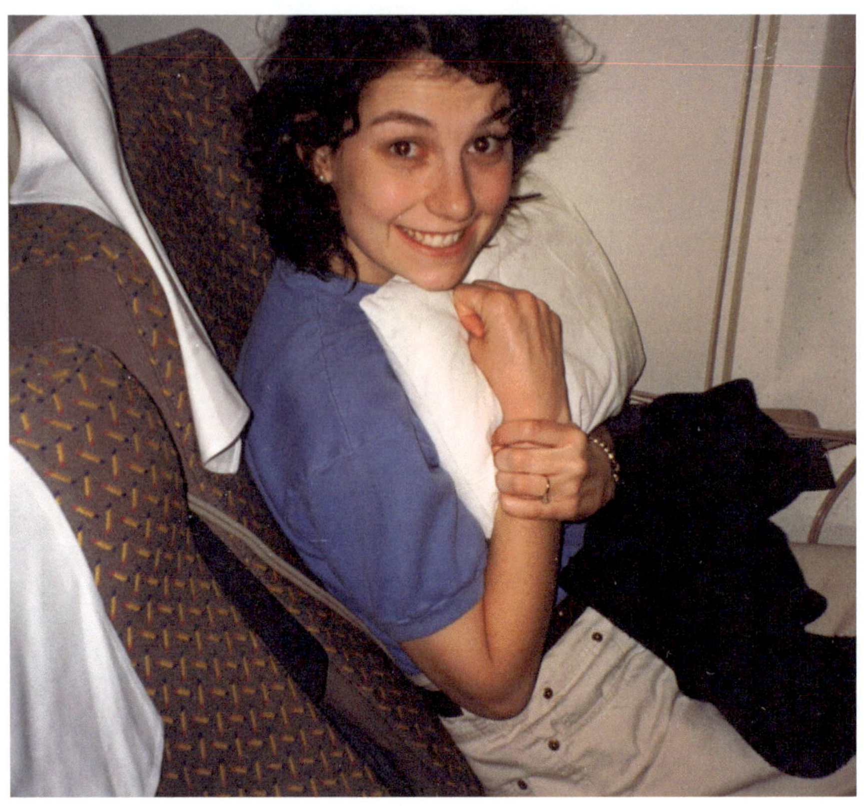

Amy getting excited for our first trip overseas to Hong Kong, Korea, and China
April 1997

CHAPTER FOURTEEN

• • • • • • • • • • • • • •

In the fall of 1996, during a trip to Charleston, Mike proposed, and Amy said yes; they were officially engaged. Lisa went dress shopping with Amy shortly after she shared the news. "She didn't gush over wedding planning or anything like that, but she was excited to be marrying Mike," Lisa said. "When she told me how he proposed, I remarked that there wasn't much fanfare, that maybe there should have been a whole, big thing, and she said, no, it was sweet, it was perfect. Whatever he did that day was perfect for the two of them."

During their hours shopping for a dress together—an outing Lisa felt honored to share—Amy wasn't sure what exactly what she wanted to wear, but she knew she didn't want anything too fancy or too expensive; money was an issue. They found a pretty, plain, lacy dress for very little cost, and Lisa talked her into buying it. Days later, Amy told Lisa she'd changed her mind. She wanted something with a little more drama. It was her only wedding, after all.

Amy's father and Judy threw the couple an engagement party in Greenville. It was Mike's first trip to visit Amy's hometown in Ohio. The party was at a park, and a friend of Mike's from college came, as well as dozens of Amy's family members, including Grandma Nisonger.

Then, in the spring of 1997, Mike and Amy took advantage of some in-kind perks from CNN advertisers to take their first overseas trip together, to Hong Kong, Korea, and China. "We could never have afforded it otherwise," said Mike.

They traveled well together from the start. They were both great flyers who could sleep anywhere. In Hong Kong, they stayed with Mike's friend Lynn from CNN in a beautiful apartment overlooking the city, which helped them feel comfortable right away. They hung out mostly on their own—and sometimes with Lynn—and went out one night with a reporter from the Wall Street Journal. There was no question that traveling suited them as a couple. "We learned we were pretty compatible," said Mike. "And we had so much fun."

In Korea, Mike got so sick he couldn't get out of bed, and they got into a big fight, but he doesn't remember what it was about. They went out to see a horrible Korean opera and visited the DMZ. In China, they took a taxi from the airport at night but weren't sure where they were going and ended up getting off at a sketchy exit and driving through a deserted area. "We thought we going to be robbed and left on the side of the road," said Mike. "But then everything ended up fine." They lived on a shoestring budget to save enough to get to the Great Wall, so in Beijing they stayed in a youth hostel with a balcony and ate on the cheap. To get to the Great Wall, they took the same bus the locals used; they were the only white people on it. Then, when they tried to use their return tickets after touring the Wall, officials told them they had to pay a second time. On principal, they refused to pay twice, so they scouted the place for Western businessmen and convinced two guys to give them a ride. After paying their entrance fee to another attraction as a way of thanking them, they ended up spending twice as second bus ticket to get back to Beijing. (This story reminded me of Amy and Maureen's antics in college, convincing people to do things they wouldn't normally be convinced to do, like ride on the back of a garbage truck.)

The following year, Amy quit her job to travel with Mike to London—their second overseas trip in three months—and they saw U2 at Wembley Stadium. After their September 1, 1997 wedding, they spent a week in Grenada for their honeymoon.

Amy and Mike met Michele Marston early in their time in Atlanta, through Amy's work, and they stayed friends through the job and home shifts. Michele's first impression of Amy was that she was bubbly—this is a descriptor I heard many, many times—and funny and very authentic.

"She had the sweetest smile. We don't remember what people say—we remember how they make us feel, and Amy always made you feel welcome and cared for. She was present, attentive, and talkative, whereas Mike was laid back."

And she never equivocated, said Michele. "She didn't hide her opinions about people or ideas, and her strongest opinions had to do with justice for disenfranchised communities—that was her focus."

Michele recalls just once or twice when Amy opened up about her family and childhood. "These things make or break a person," said Michele. "With Amy, I think her difficult childhood made her unusually strong and compassionate. Things weren't easy for her, and she grew up faster because she had to. She had a strong sense of responsibility. You can come from a broken situation and still be strong and successful—that was Amy."

From an outsider's perspective, Mike and Amy were remarkably active compared to their peers, always traveling and going out and "doing cool things," as Michele put it. During the course of their life together, Mike would evolve into the role of trip planner—Amy appreciated this immensely—but in terms of daily life, they shared the planning, energy, and enthusiasm it takes to just get out of the house and do stuff: plays, live music, festivals, movies, and dinners with friends. He was the leader when it came to moving in his work circles, and she was the leader when it came to moving in hers. Simpatico.

"We were in sync in a lot of ways," Mike told me, "as in terms of things we liked to do and traveling. We had a tradition of buying artwork on our trips, and we gravitated to the same kinds of stuff. We're similar in terms of outlook on life. She was more outgoing, no question, and I always thought of that as a good thing because she was always able to start conversations. After college, in terms of friends we hung out with, we were about even.

"We hung out alone a lot, too. We were best friends."

Amy with Chinese students in Tainanmen Square
April 1997

CHAPTER FIFTEEN

• • • • • • • • • • • • • •

Near the end of their time in Atlanta, something happened that Mike and Amy kept mostly private from friends and family: Amy was out walking alone when a man who appeared to be on drugs attacked her without provocation. Strangers pulled the man off Amy, and she was taken to the hospital. The man was arrested and convicted of aggravated assault.

"It had a major impact on her," Juliet told me about the assault. "But she always remembered that the guy was unwell—she had sympathy for him. I think the assault was one impetus for leaving Atlanta. Not a lot of topics were off limits for Amy, but I thought she gave off signals that she didn't want to talk about it, so I didn't pry."

Amy went to therapy for help healing. "She was angry," said Rachel. "She worked in the field, she knew about victimization, and she was angry that she'd become a victim. She was scared and not sleeping well, and she didn't want to be alone."

Once again, Mike and Amy packed up to move—this time to Boston, where Amy would pursue first her MBA from Boston College, then a Ph.D. in Business Administration in Organizational Behavior from Boston University. Most importantly, Boston would be the place where

Mike and Amy started their family. But the time in Atlanta working with nonprofits and disenfranchised communities had left a deep mark on Amy, one that her Madison friend Sagashus Levingston credits for ultimately pulling her toward a life and career focused on justice for women and people of color. I asked everyone I talked to when they thought Amy had been radicalized—and the answer seems to be that Amy was never not radicalized, but some combination of her mother's feminism, her experience around diverse communities in college, and her work in Atlanta coalesced to solidify Amy's life course.

MARRIAGE & FAMILY

Stay by me
And make the moment last
Please take these lips
Even if I have been kissed
A million times

—Stay by Me, Annie Lennox

Amy on her wedding day
September 1997

CHAPTER SIXTEEN

• • • • • • • • • • • • • •

Your parents married in Westchester in 1997, while they were still living in Atlanta (a couple of guests recalled that this was the week Princess Diana died; that was big news at the time) and many of their college and Atlanta friends traveled for the ceremony, bridging their worlds. Amy worked out travel logistics for friends; Warren drove with Juliet and stayed with Amy's mother, for example. It was one of the first weddings Warren had been to, and he couldn't believe they were getting married—so grown up!—but he also felt it made complete sense.

"Of course, they were going to get married," he said.

It was a simple outdoor wedding on a beautiful day. The flowers were particularly vibrant, not your typical white bouquet—Amy colors, said Rachel Van Valkenburg, a close friend from the Rape Crisis Center. Amy wore an elegant, off-white, silky dress, simple and flowing, with an open back; her colleague Florence at the Rape Crisis Center tailored it for her and added lace to the back. Mike and Amy's wedding song—the song that defined their relationship, as Mike put it—was "Stay by Me" by Annie Lennox.

Rachel recalled meeting several of Mike's high school friends among the hundred or so wedding guests—it was near their hometown, after all—but she met very few, if any, of Amy's people from before college. John, Judy, Cary, and Doug all came from Ohio but left the reception early, which might have been the only rain cloud over the otherwise happy day.

"They were perfect together," said Juliet about Amy and Mike's decision to tie the knot. "It never would have crossed my mind to think they were making a bad choice. I never questioned it. Even during the ups and downs, it was never about them being in trouble—it was always about finding a way through it together."

Amy with a group of Thai teenagers
November 2002

CHAPTER SEVENTEEN

• • • • • • • • • • • • • •

Your parents moved from Atlanta to the Boston area in January of 1999, first to Arlington, Massachusetts, then to West Roxbury, Hyde Park, and eventually Roslindale. Their return to the North gave them better access to some old friends, including Ed and Juliet Harrison, who had married around the same time, and Heather Schwoebel, who lived in Boston during a traumatic divorce—one that Amy helped her recover from.

For the first years in Boston, Amy worked for an engineering company called Teradyne as a temp in a group of 300 college recruits. She was "so awesome," and so bright and hardworking, according to her colleague and friend Lisa Koch, that she was hired full-time as a regular employee in December of that year. Amy and Lisa instantly became friends, and in August of 2002, Amy transitioned into college recruiting for the company's Human Resource Department, where Lisa already worked. Those were some tough few years for Lisa—her fiancé had passed away unexpectedly—and Amy was, in Lisa's recollection, a rock of a friend to her, a port in a storm.

"She and Mike were together for so many years before they had kids," Lisa recalled. "I was surprised when I learned how young they'd been when they met."

Amy brought a healthy, homemade lunch every day, often leftovers from the night before—it was usually Mike who cooked dinner—and she and Lisa ate together. Amy kept a case of Poland Springs water under her desk and drank room-temperature water all day long.

Lisa remembers Amy asking her if she would take a shower in Coke. "You're showering the inside of your body with Coke," she said. "You need to drink water!"

Another friend who played an important role in this era of Amy's life was Tammy Inman, whom she met through Ed and Juliet in 1999, not long after your parents landed in Boston. Before they all had kids, they spent a memorable New Year's Eve together in Somerville—they went to a party and everyone was drinking and dancing, and Tammy took a nasty spill on the slick wooden floors.

"I fell on my face and was bleeding everywhere and going into shock, and Amy and Mike put me in their car and drove me to the emergency room."

During the drive, Tammy vomited on the upholstery.

"They would not let me pay for the cleaning or detailing. I know they were reminded of that night every time the car was outside on a hot day, but they never spoke of it again, not even joking. That's what good friends they were."

Mike was kind and quiet, and Amy was expressive and extroverted—that's one consistent take from their friends. Tammy spoke with so much affection for both of them, especially Amy, who she clarified was not loud or gregarious—"though maybe sometimes she was both!"—but always warm, drew you out, and made connections.

Amy had a way—this was clear from pretty much everyone I talked to—of redirecting the spotlight away from herself, which made others feel like they were the only people on the planet when they were with her.

"She cared more about you than anything she was going through," said Lisa.

This also meant that Amy maintained an air of privacy. With Lisa, she never shared details about her family, which Lisa noticed because her own family did everything together. Lisa had the vague sense Amy wasn't close to her family, but they never discussed it. And Amy never dished about her marriage or home life, which seemed happy and under control—even their two dogs were well-behaved.

"It was her and Mike, and that was it. I sometimes envied that."

Lisa left Boston for a year, and during the time she was gone, Amy leveraged her experience in recruitment to head-up several diversity initiatives. By this time, Amy was working toward her MBA on Teradyne's dime—but with only a few classes left, she was laid off when the company downsized radically in 2002.

With Amy laid off, the couple decided to head to Thailand for Thanksgiving of 2002, and Amy was several months pregnant by spring of 2003, when she finished her MBA at Boston College. Aaron was born in August of that year, and in September, Amy started her Ph.D. at Boston University, in the organizational behavior department of the School of Management—which she decided to do, in-part, because she could be paid a stipend, and tuition would be subsidized.

Everyone who knew Amy during this time of her life—she was thirty-one years old when you were born in 2003—could plainly see how bright and capable she was. She had so much on her plate between being pregnant and pursuing her degrees, but to friends, she never seemed flustered and was always under control.

"She was one of those people who doesn't show stress, if she even felt it," said Lisa K. about those days. "Her head was on straight all of the time, and she was so smart and such a good communicator. She never stumbled, was never nervous. But she was never intimidating, either, and was always so positive, friendly, warm, and down-to-earth—who could be intimidated by that?"

Heather S. recalled thrift-store shopping with Amy to get your nursery ready.

"She picked up this rocker-recliner, and we went together to a fabric store and spent five hours making cushions one night," she remembered.

Childhood photos

College friends

Grand Canyon, December 1995

Hong Kong, May 1997

Roatán, February 2002

Thailand, November 2002

Great Wall of China, May 1997

Copan, February 2002

Amy with baby Aaron, September 2003

Jocelyn's birthday, April 16, 2006

Amy made the best Halloween costumes for the kids!
October 2006

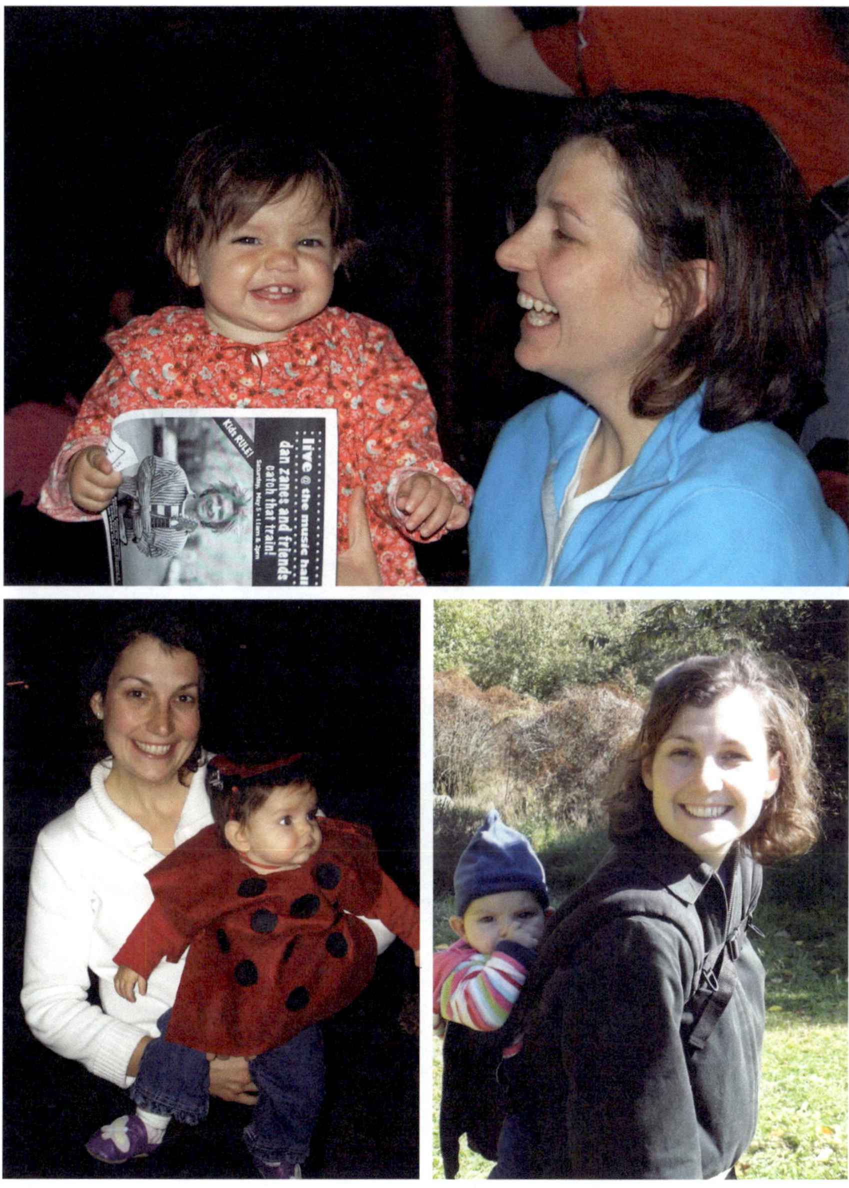

Amy with Jocelyn

Venice, April 2007

Switzerland, July 2012

Norway, July 2018

Scotland, August 2016

Selfie with Aaron

Selfie with Jocelyn

Amy at work.

Amy's M.B.A. graduation from Boston College
May 2003

CHAPTER EIGHTEEN

• • • • • • • • • • • • • •

When you were one, your parents were living in a two-family condo in Roslindale, down the street from the Arnold Arboretum, a Frederick Law Olmstead-designed park, where the bench dedicated to her and Jocelyn stands now.

In Roslindale, Amy and Mike made close, lifelong friends with several neighbors, including next-door neighbor Deb Asbrand, whose daughter Nell was your first best friend, and Jessie Jakobs, whose daughter Charlotte was yours and Nell's third wheel, as Jessie put it. Motherhood clearly suited Amy.

"Amy was Aaron's biggest fan," said Deb. "She put so much of herself into raising him. And it sounds so pedestrian, but she would be so proud of him now."

You and Nell were like brother and sister; Deb referred to the neighborhood kids as The Roslindale Crew. You were a trusting, lively kid, and you adored Nell.

"They had a lovely friendship," said Deb.

Most of the time the families spent together happened spontaneously, like walking the dogs, getting out to play, or walking to Roslindale Square for coffee. They were the kind of neighbors who could drop the kids off at each other's houses and run errands.

"It was like Sesame Street," said Jessie. "You didn't have to work hard for your friendships then. They were just always there. It was an idyllic time. We didn't realize then how idyllic it was."

Deb felt the same way.

"I still think of those days as magical moments in time, with Mike and Amy next door and Jessie across the street. The three families were so simpatico in parenting styles, we all had similar outlooks, and the kids were the same age. We had a lot of dinners together. It was so easy, an overly perfect moment in time. I was a single mother, and having those friendships meant a lot to me," said Deb.

Amy became known as the one who would always whip up a big casserole at the last minute, and Mike was always tending the grill; they always invited people in, no matter what. She and Mike hosted Easter dinner, and Deb would make a ham. Mike and Amy were transplants and didn't have family nearby, so the neighborhood took the place of family. Jessie knew Amy wasn't close to her family, mostly because she had so little in common with them.

"She had a worldly outlook," said Jessie. "Travel was their main thing. She wasn't into stuff, didn't wear fancy clothes or makeup, or drive nice cars. If it was frivolous, she didn't care about it. She put money into picture frames and art they collected—that was like furniture to her," said Jessie.

And the trips! Three trips abroad the year they were married, followed by more when you were still in arms. Travel planning was one of the times when Amy let go and left the planning to Mike.

"I have the sense that she was the idea person," said Juliet about the family's impressive travel. "And Mike made it happen."

The friends spent a lot of time talking about public schools, which were assigned on a lottery system. And when Amy hosted birthday parties, she had guests bring wrapped books to give out as favors.

"She always had creative ideas for birthdays, always made their cakes, and her parties were homegrown and organic," said Jessie, who recalled that Charlotte was stung by a bee in the backyard at one of your early birthdays.

The first year Amy and Mike lived in Roslindale, Deb hosted an Easter egg hunt in her backyard, and then in subsequent years, the three moms filled dozens of plastic eggs, and the dads hid them in the arboretum, then all three families walked down and let the kids run around hunting. "It was a beautiful tradition," said Deb. "Amy made a video from the photos of those hunts. She had a nice camera, and she was a great photographer." Deb recalled specifically that despite everything she had going on, Amy had spent time making the DVD and the label. Where did she find the energy?

Amy was also the one who organized the neighborhood yard sales, once in the spring and once in the fall—a huge amount of work but a community builder, and building community was Amy's specialty.

The families also trick-or-treated together. Amy always made her kids' costumes, including a lion outfit for Aaron one year, and an elephant another year; she used a vacuum cleaner hose for the elephant's trunk.

"She was creative," said Deb. "But she was more into doing stuff with her kids than feathering her nest. Decorating wasn't her thing. She cared more that her kids were comfortable and had places to play and run around in the house. She was very casual about cleanliness—Amy knew her priorities and values."

Amy and Aaron on the beach in St. John
March 2005

CHAPTER NINETEEN

• • • • • • • • • • • • • •

After you were born, Lisa Koch and Amy spent a good deal of time together, usually in a park, and Lisa admired Amy's calm handling of this brand-new baby, who was, Lisa recalled, super cute. Once, with Lisa and Amy chatting nearby, you fell off the jungle gym.

"Amy was calm, always calm. She strolled over, picked Aaron up, and never panicked. Everything she did, she did well," said Lisa.

When Lisa had her own baby, Justin, in May of 2009, Amy bought him a hooded baby towel with his name embroidered on it, each letter made from a different animal. Eleven years later, Lisa sent Amy a photo of Justin wearing that baby towel on his head. But the women lost touch—except for Christmas cards—in the years before Amy's accident.

Lisa is still in Human Resources, and now she has her Masters of Science in Management—something she pursued one year after her fiancé died, at least partly because of Amy's steady support and encouragement.

"I lost a year of my life when my fiancé died. Then something clicked in me, and I knew I needed to do something just for me. That was Amy's voice in my head."

Amy carrying a sleepy Aaron in Venice
April 2007

CHAPTER TWENTY

• • • • • • • • • • • • • •

Amy was always certain she wanted a second child. When she went into labor with Jocelyn on April 15, 2006, Deb took care of you while your parents went to the hospital. Amy gave her a fleece blanket as a thank you gift, which Deb still owns today.

"We had these three little rascals," said Jessie of the neighborhood kids. "Then Jocelyn came along and there was one more."

Jocelyn came out ready to occupy as much of the world as it could handle.

"Jocelyn was plucky from the get-go," said Deb. "She was no younger-sister-shrinking-violet. She stepped right out on stage and got into the thick of things. She never held back."

But Amy was sensitive to the fact that Jocelyn was the youngest and always made sure she was included among the neighborhood gang. Once, Charlotte referred to Jocelyn—nicely—as a baby, and Amy said, "She's not a baby—she's a toddler."

Mothers often refer to their kids as babies, but Amy was the opposite. She wanted her kids to be independent and spirited and take risks.

"She was a planner and caretaker, but her parenting style was laid back," said Jessie. "We'd be in the arboretum, and the kids would put something in their mouths or climb on this huge half dome, and she would just let them and never freak out. I admired how they took their kids traveling so early on—they did it all. Our generation tends to hover, but her parenting style was all about cultivating independence. She did not micromanage."

Not all mothers—even very good ones—come to parenthood naturally, but Amy's friends from Boston all agree that Amy seemed to inhabit the role gracefully, without fuss. "She was a doting mother, unforced and authentic," said Tammy. "It seemed effortless for her. It was so good for me to have her as a model and to get tips from her—she approached it all with an open mind. I would get flustered when the kids had tantrums, but she was always patient and measured."

Which is not to say she was immune to frustration, but no one could remember a time when she lost her cool. The era of raising young kids is a challenging one in any family, though, and Mike recalls his own patience running out regularly, even if Amy's rarely did.

"We tried to share the nighttime stuff," he said about the many feedings and wakings, "but Amy was much better at it, because I'm not great at getting up in the middle of the night."

Jessie was one of several friends who looked to Amy as a model when it came to parenting and more.

"She had a way about her that was so confident," said Jessie. "You didn't question her because she was always doing the right thing and was always the most rational and logical person in the room. She cared about people, but she never cared what people thought of her."

Tammy Inman, too, talked about how she looked to Amy for guidance, even when she didn't quite know she was doing so.

"In friendship and in motherhood, she had a mature perspective on life and a way of reframing a situation to help you see the bigger picture—with love and without judgment. Sometimes I knew when it was happening, and sometimes I realized later.

"I don't know where she got this ability, but it was something special."

When living in Boston, we took a day trip to Martha's Vineyard
each summer.
July 2006

CHAPTER TWENTY-ONE

• • • • • • • • • • • • • •

Several people who knew your mother when you and Jocelyn were small noted that not only was Amy a natural mother, but she was also committed to being a good mother and pursued motherhood in a way that was almost academic.

Juliet Harrison said, "She worried about raising a boy who was well adjusted and secure, and also feminist and conscious. She was always the mom who hosted playdates and planned activities, like flash cards or potato printing. It wasn't really her nature to be so deliberate, organized, and serious about raising children—she was more silly, fun, and sweet otherwise. But she was a good study."

Juliet and Amy spent much of the early part of motherhood together: Jacob was your age, and Colin was one year younger than Jocelyn. In 2005, when you and Jacob were still tiny and Colin and Jocelyn hadn't come along, the two families rented a house on Saint John together. On Tuesdays, Juliet and Jacob spent time with Amy and you, and later Jocelyn and Colin, either at the park or the city pool, and Juliet recalled that Amy bonded with Jacob easily and organically—they both loved red grapes.

"Building connections was her natural state—not the effortful exercises around teaching kids. She liked kids just as she liked adults and made them feel comfortable," said Juliet.

Tammy Inman, who had kids around the same age, joined the Tuesday crew and recalled those days fondly.

"We did playdates, and the ladies got together for a meal every month or two. We bonded over new motherhood. It was invaluable having that support," said Tammy.

Your mother was clearly captivated by you both. She was always involved and active, on the playground or on playdates, despite everything else that required her energy. "She was so tuned into her kids," said Tammy. "I remember her talking so lovingly about how bright and curious Aaron was, and how energetic and fearless Jocelyn was."

Deb recalls Amy's parenting style as being very deliberate and thoughtful, with less of the free-floating anxiety many new parents experience.

"Amy loved motherhood as much as I did," said Deb. "Some of my favorite memories are of us sitting on the grass in my backyard while the kids played. It was lovely. We talked a lot, and I remember Amy had a lot of curiosity about other people, a lot of empathy. It was easy to connect with her. One day, I shared my adoption story, and I told her the details, about waiting and waiting to go to Cambodia. She was moved."

It didn't surprise Deb, given their history together, that Amy went on to create Doyenne, which is essentially a support network—she knew firsthand how it felt to be supported by Amy.

"She was very directed about motherhood," said Deb. "I had insecurities, like a lot of women. She gave everything a lot of thought, with the goal of establishing a nurturing, supportive home. She was unwavering. I rarely saw her frustrated. She struck me as one of these people who was exactly where she wanted to be. She was naturally calm and centered. She knew she wanted to have a happy marriage and home. Plus, they had the two dogs! She amazed me, with all that was going on in her life such as the dissertation, the kids, and the marriage."

The dogs! Sander and Berkeley. Amy loved them and was dedicated to walking them.

"I have an image of her in my mind with the leashes attached to her waist, pushing the stroller, and chatting with people. That was like her sanctuary, her natural state," said Jessie.

Amy was thrilled to have a second baby, but a little jarred by how different you and Jocelyn were at a young age. You were a cautious, calm child—but Jocelyn was fearless. If she could see it, she would climb it.

"We'd turn around at the park and Joce would be on top of the jungle gym," said Juliet. "'I can't keep her on the ground,' Amy would say."

Jocelyn was always climbing trees. "She was a monkey," said Jessie.

Tammy said, "Jocelyn was always the first to the top of whatever, even when she was the littlest. She was coming into her own when they left Boston, but I had no doubt she would be a force."

Many parents have an easier time with the second child; they relax a little bit.

"Amy always seemed confident, but when Jocelyn came along, she became even more so," said Juliet.

Amy and Aaron at the pumpkin patch
October 2006

CHAPTER TWENTY-TWO

• • • • • • • • • • • • • •

Amy was super friendly and always smiling, said her friends. Warm, inviting, easy to talk to, and open but not particularly confessional.

"We hit it off right away," Deb said. "Amy was very empathic. I always thought I could see the midwestern quality in her, a wholesome sensibility. She was so beautiful, with her creamy pale complexion and curly, chocolate-brown hair, and she had a sweet nature. She was down to earth and thoughtful. She was really solid."

Deb, too, knew little of Amy's childhood, although the two spent a lot of time together.

"Amy alluded to a difficult childhood but never talked about it explicitly," said Deb. "I'll say that I always understood she was committed to establishing a stable family life. She came from a background of divorce and instability—it was always clear to me that having a healthy, well-adjusted family life was really important to her. But I never asked for details about her childhood, and I don't think she wanted to talk about it."

The other Roslindale women knew only a little about Amy's mother.

"Amy didn't share too much," said Jessie. "You could get close, but she was protective about what she shared. She talked about her mother's beauty and her men, though.

"Amy was beautiful, too, but didn't define herself that way."

She radiated empathy and positivity. "She always had a kind word or helping hand," said Tammy. "She always looked you in the eye and cared about what you were saying. She always paused to think before making an insightful response. She was an extremely caring person."

Like most of Amy's friends, Tammy didn't push her to divulge her past, mostly because she recognized that Amy valued her privacy, and she didn't want to intrude. She had the sense that her childhood had been challenging but nothing more. Tammy noted, too, that although in the group they'd formed around playdates, there were always a couple of women venting about their marriages, but Amy never did.

"She was never one to blithely complain or air dirty laundry," said Tammy. "I didn't know Mike well, but he struck me as the strong, silent type. He didn't say a lot, but he had a great sense of humor, that was clear right away. Their marriage was strong, and it always struck me as a mature marriage, like they'd been married for a long time."

Heather Schwoebel, too, mentioned that Amy didn't discuss her marriage with her friends. "As much as she was giving and warm, she was also private," she said.

On vacation at Acadia National Park
August 2008

CHAPTER TWENTY-THREE

• • • • • • • • • • • • • •

Of their many close Boston friends, Amy opened up about her childhood and marriage most to Ed and Juliet. This might have been because she and Juliet shared similar upbringings.

"We both grew up with very little parental support and were pretty independent. Maybe it seemed like we were young to get married at age twenty-five, but we both had experience that allowed us to know the difference between a partner and a temporary fling. We had the benefit of maturity that a lot of twenty-five-year-olds don't have," said Juliet.

Juliet knew that there was a lot in Amy's childhood that was out of her control, an above-average amount of scary chaos.

"Maybe as a new adult, she wanted to try to control life or at least put up guardrails," Juliet said. "In so many ways, Amy's adult life was completely different from her mother's."

In Boston, Amy went to work researching her mother's disorder, and she went to therapy to discuss it with someone who could help her understand.

"This was how she dealt with things," said Juliet. "She learned about them."

When Amy was frustrated—and only the closest friends ever saw Amy's rare temper—she argued with Mike and got sarcastic and impatient, but she always maintained control. She was particularly motivated to learn about herself and her loved ones—so when she and Mike hit a rough patch, she threw herself into figuring a solution.

Jessie recalled Amy confiding about the marriage during this time. She was failing to connect emotionally with Mike, who had trouble recognizing when she was going through something.

"She wanted a closer connection," said Jessie. "She had an emotional side, and she knew they could work through it."

Eventually, with Amy's encouragement, Mike received an ADHD diagnosis. He started to exercise more and began to recognize some of the ways he was inhibiting their closeness.

"He got it together with her help," said Jessie admiringly.

Amy shared about this rough patch with Ed and Juliet, too, who recall Amy's curiosity and determination.

"Here Mike had the new part of his identity that affected their relationship, and she was very open about the process of learning and adjusting and about what it meant for their marriage. Very little was a closed topic with Amy," said Juliet.

Ed told me a story that has occupied a piece of his mind for twenty years. In 1998, long before they had children, the two couples met up in San Francisco for four days; this was while your parents were still living in Atlanta and before Amy's assault. One night, the foursome were out at a bar, drinking and playing pool, and Amy was talking about men behaving badly, being entitled, and diminishing women in the workplace and out of it. Ed was offended. "She was always so calming and friendly, quiet at first, cerebral, always observing and analyzing. This was the first time I saw that she had an edge to her."

Amy apologized for offending him. Today, understanding what he does about male privilege and the patriarchy, Ed regrets the reaction he'd been so quick to defend back then.

"I wish I could go back and validate what she was saying," he said.

Unlike the friends Amy made in her Madison years, Ed and Juliet witnessed Amy grow and mature over decades, from a college student to an academic to an entrepreneur.

"She was always comfortable in her own skin," said Juliet, "but in her last ten years, she blossomed."

Juliet and Ed remember Amy as fun and goofy and also serious.

"She could always go there—she could talk about something intense and personal, then flip to being giddy and silly," said Juliet.

The seeds of her work with women and people of color were planted early in Amy, possibly before Ed and Juliet even met her, but they grew during her years at Teradyne, and then during her Ph.D. work around barriers to entrepreneurship. Over the years, friends watched her develop into the woman she was at the time of her passing.

"She was so independent, so self-made," said Juliet. "She was worldly and also a 4-H girl from the state fair. And she loved her kids to death. They were everything."

Deb also shared something she learned from Amy all those years ago, which she keeps in mind to this day. Amy spent a lot of time at a cafe, working on her dissertation, and she told Deb that even if she only wrote one paragraph, she was moving forward. One step at a time. As a writer, Deb knows that there's a world of difference between one paragraph and a blank page.

"Even one paragraph is progress," said Deb.

Deb saw in Amy, even without the benefit of hindsight, that while most of us are making it up as we go along, Amy had a life plan. She knew that the perfect was the enemy of the good, and she never expressed any ambiguity about her career. She always knew where she was headed.

"There was a certain kind of perfectionism in her," said Deb, "but she knew when and where to apply it. She was disciplined and systematic in a lot of ways, including the division of labor in their home."

Heather S. shared a couple of Amy stories that have stayed in her brain all of these years. She'd just left a bad marriage when she reunited in Boston with Mike and Amy, and Mike admitted to her that they'd never liked her husband.

"I was flattered that they had been willing to put up with him to hang out with me!" she said.

Heather babysat you when you were small. "I had no idea what I was doing," she said. "I put this nine-month-old baby in a laundry basket and carried him around. I met Jocelyn the day they came home from the hospital; she was this little nugget in Aaron's hand-me-downs."

Once, Heather and Amy were hanging out, and Amy parked her car in the driveway with you and Jocelyn strapped into your car seats, then she went inside to grab an umbrella. When she came back outside, she found that the car had rolled down the driveway and hit the garage door. You were both fine, of course, but it rattled Amy (and not much did).

"I calmed her, and the kids were fine," said Heather. "She drank a beer and got past it in about twenty minutes. She had experience being the only adult in the room, from her childhood, and you could see that she knew how to soothe herself."

Years later, after you and Jocelyn were both on the scene, Heather and her second husband asked Amy and Mike to be the guardians of their kids. This was before they'd decided to move to Madison. Heather remembers popping the question one night over Thai food, and their answer was yes.

"They'd already been together for twenty years by that point," said Heather. "We trusted them completely."

In their years as neighbors and friends, the Roslindale women knew Amy as more likely to step in to help out than to ask others for help.

"She was subtly stubborn, and she was an expert in everything, probably because she raised herself a lot of the time, got herself out of her hometown and off to college. She was fiercely independent," said Jessie.

Maybe she wasn't comfortable seeking help—but she was excellent in a crisis. She knew what to do and did it. One night, near the end of the family's time in Boston, Jessie called her late. Jessie's kids—Charlotte was five, and her son was just an infant—were asleep, but the police were on their way because Jessie's then-husband had attacked her in a psychotic episode.

"I thought I was going to die," Jessie said. "Amy was the first person I called after I contacted the police. She came right over, and it was like she had a checklist in her brain. She said, 'Give me the kids, we're having a sleepover.' She wasn't my best friend, but she had this innate ability to help, and we trusted each other.

"She saved me that night."

Tammy, too, knew firsthand how it felt to receive Amy's generous help. When she was diagnosed with breast cancer, Tammy had one kiddo in kindergarten and one potty training, and it was Amy who drove half an hour each way to bring her meals, and she even took the kids for a whole day at the beach.

"Some people don't know what to do, and I understand that. Even my family didn't know how to help sometimes. But Amy knew exactly what to do, and she did it with a smile, without making a fuss or expecting anything."

On vacation in the White Mountains in July 2009

CHAPTER TWENTY-FOUR

• • • • • • • • • • • • • •

During her years in the Ph.D. program, Amy focused mostly on qualitative research, which means she interviewed entrepreneurs. It was a type of research, her colleagues told me, that suited her personality.

"With qualitative research, you get to talk to people firsthand about their journeys and experiences. Amy was a great interviewer. It's not easy to talk about your struggles as a minority entrepreneur, but Amy got people to open up," said Elana Feldman, who was three years behind Amy in the doctoral program.

Amy was a mentor to Elana. She showed her around when she arrived, and was warm, supportive, and authentic.

"Once you got to know Amy, she could be really hilarious—she told jokes with a poker face and made me laugh and laugh," said Elana.

Amy was stretched thin at that time, trying to finish her dissertation with two young kids at home—Mike and Amy hired a nanny for the first years, then you both went to daycare—and there was a lot of pressure to land a top research job.

But Amy knew what she wanted: she was going to teach, not chase bylines.

"She was at peace with doing what made her and her family happy," said Elana.

Jina Mao, who shared workspace with Elana and Amy, recalled how easy Amy made it seem to juggle the demands of an academic career with young children.

"She had a very strong inner voice," said Jina. "She listened to her heart."

Jina credits Amy for being the first person to make her feel confident about what she offered in the program. The two were walking together one day, and Amy stopped and gave Jina a compliment on her work.

"I was so moved," said Jina, "because as early Ph.D. students, we were all insecure about our capabilities. There were so many smart people around us. But Amy calmed me down and made me feel like I had something to offer. When she sees you're hurt or insecure, she's the first person to take care of you."

A third member of Amy's Ph.D. cohort was Yan Shen, who remembers Amy as warm-hearted, considerate, and kind.

"She was always cheerful and gave off a lot of positive energy. She truly enjoyed life. She knew what she wanted and was strongly self-aware. She had a passion and pursued it. I really admired her."

All three women talked about Amy's quick mind and high energy when it came to good ideas.

"She made brainstorming fun," said Elana.

Doyenne, which at this point was still a decade in the future, was the natural result of the passionate research Amy pursued while earning her Ph.D. She left academia, but she returned to the work with minority entrepreneurs that had fueled her dissertation years earlier.

"She didn't take the typical academic path that BU wanted students to take. She had clear goals and studied the people and ideas she wanted to study," said Elana.

Women in academia, especially mothers, sometimes choose to keep their work and home lives separate—but that wasn't Amy's style. She talked constantly about her kids, and her colleagues felt they knew you and Jocelyn even though they didn't meet you in person. Amy talked a lot about climbing into your bed in the mornings and talking with you and realizing that you were dealing with things she couldn't make go away, like problems with friends and school.

"She loved being with her kids and hated rushing out the door," said Elana. "It was clear from her actions how she prioritized her kids, even though she was also really passionate about her work."

The desire to be two places at once might have something to do with the many parking tickets she racked up around BU during these years. Amy was notorious for always running late—almost everyone I talked to mentioned this—and equally admired for never letting time constraints rule her life.

"She didn't worry about being late," said Jessie. "She didn't get stressed about it."

Years later, one of her Edgewood students and friends, Annette Miller, echoed this observation.

"She was not a time-centered person. A conversation continued as long as it needed to. Life was about connecting for Amy," she said.

In December of 2010, Amy successfully defended her dissertation to a packed room of friends and colleagues, which was fairly uncommon.

"The large audience was a reflection of the community Amy built," said Elana.

After Amy finished her Ph.D. and moved to Madison, she took the lead in keeping up with her former cohort via Skype. Shortly after the move, she took a side trip to Finland while the family was traveling in Europe, to help present a paper. Elana met her there. Amy was a great travel companion, easygoing and always smiling.

"She had the ability to be in the moment and enjoy life," said Elana. "We went to this big party and were talking to people we just met, and I remember Amy was so comfortable just talking to anyone—strangers from all around Europe. Walking home at midnight, the sun was bright and weird, and we were so happy to be part of this big academic nerd party. I'll always remember that."

Amy's eventual decision to leave academia couldn't have been an easy one. She was a gifted researcher by all accounts, heavily invested and observant, with an eye for details and context. And to Amy, the work was personal as well as professional.

Deb recalls Amy telling her about being at the park during the day with the kids and other young moms and realizing that none of the other moms knew she was a Ph.D. student.

"She described this kind of transition where if you're a mom with two kids and you're facing that decision of whether to go back to work or put your career on hold—or have a third kid and stay home—her research dovetailed with all of it."

Jessie was similarly struck by Amy's dedication to her work.

"She was stubborn but not a pain in the neck," she said. "You could not take advantage of her. She had such a solid head on her shoulders, and she was such a hard worker. She was wholly dedicated to social justice and getting marginalized people into business and entrepreneurship. She was determined to give them a voice."

Like others, Jessie assumed this passion for social justice developed during Amy's years working at the Rape Crisis Center in Atlanta, only a year or two out of college.

"To me, business school seemed like an odd choice for Amy—but then again, she was there to bridge the gap between those who had voices and those who did not. She wanted to help people, and she loved good ideas," said Jessie.

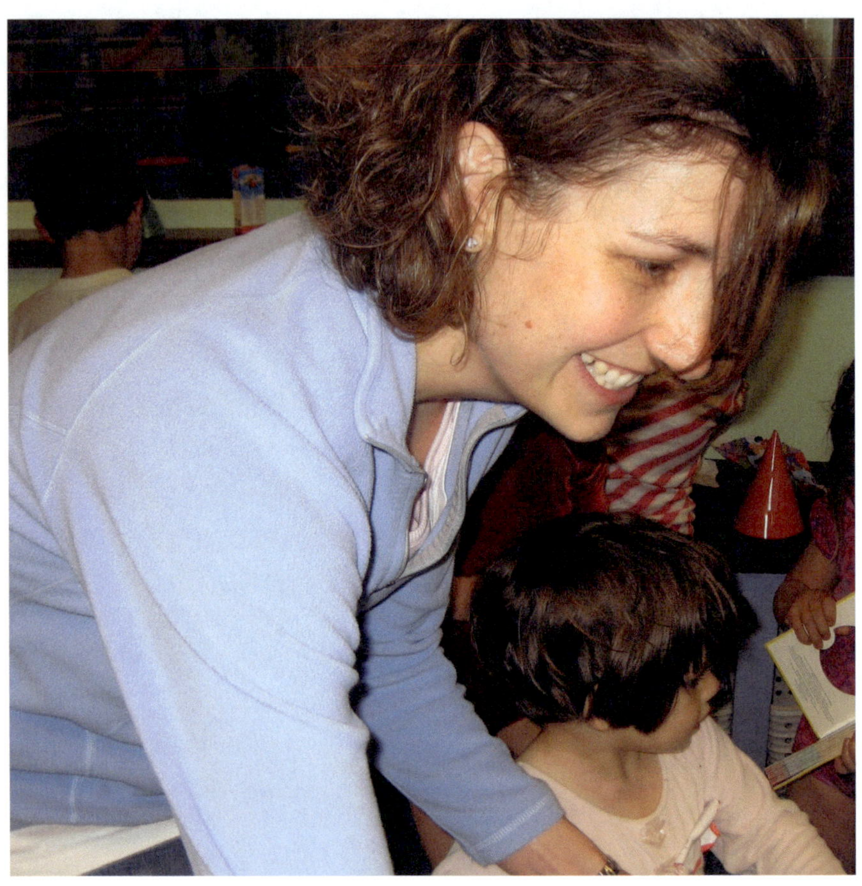

One of my favorite photos of Amy at Jocelyn's 4th birthday party.
When the kids were little, we had book exchanges at their birthday parties.
Amy is passing out wrapped books to Jocelyn's friends.
April 2010

CHAPTER TWENTY-FIVE

Mike and Amy never seriously considered having a third child.

"Amy's motor was running," said Deb. "She was always making plans for where they were headed next."

She gave Heather Schwoebel all your hand-me-down clothes before Heather was even pregnant.

"She had a plan," said Heather.

And where she was headed next was, in 2010, to Madison, to take an assistant professor position in the business school at Edgewood College.

"We all figured she'd be promoted to Dean of Edgewood in no time," said Jessie. "Then President."

The night before your family moved to Madison, Jocelyn fell from the swings in Deb's backyard and broke her arm. The families were all grilling and hanging out, and Jocelyn—who was already falling in love with gymnastics at four years old—took a spill.

"Jocelyn was always raring to go," said Jessie. "She took after Amy. She always kept up with the bigger kids, but she was also very independent and physically active."

It was a stressful time even without the last-minute crisis, and Deb wondered how Amy was holding it all together. "She really had enormous strength," said Deb.

Tammy and Amy stayed in touch for several years then drifted apart. "I missed her," said Tammy. "I always figured we'd pick up where we left off when we saw each other again. She was one of a kind. I have other friends, but she was special. It's difficult to lose her. But it's been healing to read and learn about everything Amy meant to the Madison community. It's inspirational to see that side of her. Even though she's gone, I try to focus on how she made the world better."

Deb, too, read the coverage of the accident, and had no trouble connecting the younger woman she'd known so well with the successful woman Amy had become. She remembered that a couple of years after the family moved to Madison, they'd returned for a visit, and you had conveyed that you missed Boston and didn't like Madison.

"Madison was Amy's adventure," said Deb. "Boston was her runway. Here, she was still in her formative years, and the kids were so young and demanded so much of her time, and she was so involved in her dissertation. Once she graduated and got the post at Edgewood, a new life started for her. She really flourished there."

At the memorial in Madison, Amy's old Roslindale neighbors came face-to-face with how much Amy had grown, and how widespread her impact had become since they'd first known her back in Boston.

"So many people showed up to remember her," said Jessie. "She had really carved out a place. She did that everywhere she went."

It was clear that the choices Amy made so deliberately had turned out to be good ones. In Madison, she'd made a life where she was happy, energized, successful, and enthusiastic. She'd blossomed.

Amy's Doctorial graduation from Boston University
May 2010

CHAPTER TWENTY-SIX

• • • • • • • • • • • • • •

Cary, the younger of Amy's two half-brothers by fifteen months, was the only person in Amy's family of origin who shared Amy's urge to travel. When she led trips to Malawi through Edgewood's nursing program, Cary joined her twice—he was the only guy on both trips, which focused on women's empowerment and took the group to different villages all over Malawi.

"Watching her work with women helped me know her better," Cary told me. "We weren't raised in the same household, and she has a different mom. I was raised in church, conservatively, and she didn't agree with a lot of what I was taught to believe. But over time, it was clear to us both that my thinking was more in line with hers than our other siblings."

Cary's memories of Amy go as far back as when he was seven or eight years old, when she was already in college. She visited John and Judy's house for a week each Christmas, but otherwise Cary never lived with her on a daily basis.

"I was so excited whenever she was coming to visit. I remember going to the airport and picking her up and wishing she could stay longer," he said.

They went bowling and spent time together when she was visiting, and this was a highlight of Cary's year. Amy brought him and their brother Rob gifts from the places she'd visited, and once she made Cary a list of words in Spanish, which he used—he thought it was so cool.

"Amy allowed me to think that traveling and seeing the world was something you could do on your own terms. You don't have to do life the way you're expected to," he said.

When Amy was in her first year at American, John and Judy brought the boys to D.C. for a visit. She was still living in the dorms, and Rob and Cary stayed with her.

"That was the first time I saw a homeless person," said Cary. "We were going to decorate a door for someone's birthday, in the design of a table with placemats and a cake, and we were getting supplies, and we saw this guy on the street. At the time I didn't even realize there was such a thing as homelessness in this country."

Cary asked Amy about it, and she explained.

"Being from the Midwest, and being raised in church, sometimes you get those old ideas stuck inside you. My mother's mother was racially insensitive, and everyone I knew used words I wouldn't use now," said Cary. Cary has moved deliberately away from this thinking in his adult life, partly due to Amy's influence.

Once, when Amy was visiting Ohio and driving the boys to the county fair, where they both had 4-H projects in competition, Cary used a term he'd heard for knocking on someone's door and running away, and Amy pulled the car over and took him to task for it. She was shocked and concerned and explained what the word means and how it affects others.

"Amy was the first person to tell me I shouldn't use that word and why," said Cary.

When she visited her father and Judy's house overnight, Amy slept on the couch. The boys shared a room, and at night, the kids would all watch Christmas movies.

When Cary was a junior in high school, he visited Amy and Mike in Atlanta, and the following year, he visited them in Boston after they moved.

"We talked a lot about her relationship with our father, how she never saw much of him while she was growing up. It was so different for me. For me, he was always there, and I never went through divorce. He was twenty when she was born and thirty when I was born, which I guess made all the difference," said Cary.

In 1996, the family came to New York for Amy and Mike's wedding but left the reception early to get back to Ohio for one of Rob's soccer games. "Having your father leave your wedding early is not an easy thing—it hurt her a lot," Cary said.

But other than his talks with Amy, the family didn't discuss difficult or emotional stuff. "I just always believed my father hated his ex-wife, but he didn't tell me that. I come from a long line of avoiding emotions," he said.

Cary works in local government today in Florida, and sometimes, he struggles with his desire to make a difference in peoples' lives. This desire, he said, came from Amy, who was the first person to open his eyes to how easy his life had been. She helped him realize how many peoples' lives aren't easy, especially if they're not white and male.

"Amy gave me a way out of the echo chamber. For me, wanting to travel also satisfies that desire to see different ways of living and doing things. She gave me so much advice, but I never felt criticized or judged by her. She was always that way—effortlessly nurturing—from the beginning to the end," he said.

Where Amy was outgoing, sociable, and at ease in a room of strangers, Cary struggles with confidence. When he confided in Amy that he was seeing a therapist, she encouraged him. "It never hurts to see a therapist," she told him. Cary looked at what Amy accomplished and set higher standards for himself as a result. When she pushed him to apply for a supervisory position, he took her advice and got it.

"Maybe I idolized her a little," Cary said. "Everyone has failures in their past, but I never saw hers. At the end of the day, her goal wasn't to make money but to help women, and that's what she was doing."

PART FIVE

MADISON

"Women are not broken."

—Amy

On vacation in Paris
July 2012

CHAPTER TWENTY-SEVEN

• • • • • • • • • • • • • •

While it's true that by the end of her ten years at Edgewood, Amy was worn down by the many aspects of academia, and the college itself, which both resisted Amy's brand of disruption and change, it's also true that Amy found her footing in Madison right away. This was at least partly because she was doing what she did best: teaching, mentoring, empowering people, and getting them excited about their own ideas. In the classroom, Amy ran a tight ship and left no room for complacence. There was no hiding in her class—if students didn't speak up, she called them out and engaged them.

Kacie Conroy met Amy in 2009, when Amy was new to Edgewood, and Kacie was just starting her master's program. Kacie was interested in startups and entrepreneurship—Amy's wheelhouse—but the entrepreneurship classes had a tendency not to fill, so Kacie and Amy engaged in independent study.

"The first thing you noticed about Amy was her arms," said Kacie. "They were like the arms of one of those inflatable figures people use for advertising on the side of the road. I think of her every time I see one of those things."

Amy was energetic, even flamboyant. Kacie knew right away that she had hit the mentor jackpot.

"You got a wedge into a relationship with Amy—for me that wedge was Edgewood—and then she brought you all the way in, the whole person. She was my professor, my mentor, my friend. She melded worlds very quickly," said Kacie.

When Kacie announced her own pregnancy during one of their meetings, Amy turned from mentor to cheerleader.

"She did the arms," said Kacie. "She said, 'I love kids!'"

And she wasn't just saying that to be friendly. After Kacie had her baby, Callum, Amy told her to bring him to a catch-up meeting at a cafe, then gathered him up in her arms and walked around, talking to people while holding him, cheerful as could be.

"She always said motherhood was her favorite role," said Kacie.

Over the years, she and Kacie met over drinks or a meal to brainstorm Kacie's work and Amy's. They went to Barriques on Monroe Street or a French place on the Square, and Amy always ordered healthy—a salad, usually, and sometimes a cocktail.

"Amy was all about fun. She always wanted to treat me, but I made sure we traded off. She always made you feel like the only person in the room."

With Kacie and in general, Amy's focus was on diversity and inclusion, and it was her ability to connect with people that made her ideals into reality. Years later, when Amy was preparing to leave Edgewood, she invited Kacie to sit on the advisory board for the College of Business.

"She got me a seat at the table. Sometimes that's all someone needs, an introduction and a seat at the table," said Kacie.

From Amy, Kacie learned to prioritize inclusion first, followed by diversity, because you can't bring in people if they don't fit. Kacie now includes others the way Amy included her.

"Her point was that you have to create a community of belonging first, so people stay and feel valued," said Kacie.

The tables turned at one point: Kacie invited Amy to speak at an inclusion and diversity meeting at her corporate firm. She knew Amy to be a passionate and energetic speaker, wholly engaged and dynamic.

"When she got on her soapbox, it happened quick—like a train taking off," said Kacie. "You'd almost have to be as demonstrative as she was to get her to pause."

During the meeting, Amy showed up just like she did in committee meetings or the classroom, with her super high energy, wild gestures, and large presence, zigzagging all over the room.

"She probably got in a million steps a day," said Kacie. "She never stopped moving."

At some point, Kacie looked around and saw that her colleagues seemed shell-shocked, like they were drinking from a firehose.

"I stopped her so people could ask questions," she said. "Within a few minutes, they got it. She did this thing where she just dropped knowledge on you. Most of the time, it was common sense, but she had a way of putting two and two together. It's what made her such a good professor."

At their last meeting, a month before she was gone, Amy talked to Kacie about her children, and you in particular, Aaron. She told Kacie about your entrepreneurial spirit and your side hustle. She was impressed; it sounded like you had a lot of your mother in you.

"She laughed and said that if anyone can make something work, it was Aaron," said Kacie. "She wanted to be his start-up mentor."

Kacie felt at the time like she must have been one of a hundred people connected to Amy, and was baffled at how Amy managed to be so generous with her time.

"She was always working, and Mike traveled a lot—I would love to sneak a peek at her calendar," said Kacie. "I don't know how, but she always found time to meet with me."

Carrie Sanders met Amy in early 2015, after Amy was picked to become interim dean of the School of Business, a position she would hold for two years, until she left Edgewood to make a full-time go of Doyenne. Carrie was an adjunct teacher, and Amy invited her to take over a course she'd created around business innovation.

"It was a complete disaster of a class," said Carrie. She went to Amy with her desperation on her sleeve. "I said to her, 'What do you do when the kids obviously do not want to be in class?'"

Amy sat Carrie down. "I get in their faces and shut their laptops," Amy told her.

Carrie was floored. Amy had a presence and confidence she didn't know if she could muster for herself.

"She was feared and loved by students," she said. "And by me."

Over time, Amy's reassurance and advice helped make Carrie a better teacher. She learned social impact from Amy, and now she teaches it to others—a ripple effect that outlasts Amy's life.

After Doyenne started, several of Carrie's students reported that they'd taken a class with Amy there and raved about it, so Carrie took it, too. It was called Entrepreneurship for Good, and Amy held the class in the Doyenne offices. "It was a small cohort, and the point was to take entrepreneurs with messy ideas and hone them until, by the end of the semester, we had something to invest in. An enterprise idea," said Carrie.

Carrie could see clearly how Edgewood wasn't a good fit for Amy, in the long run.

"She was ahead of her time and looking to disrupt structures. She brought in new teaching styles and new ideas. The institution was not ready for her," said Carrie.

When Amy taught, Carrie recalled, she came to class carrying a little moleskin notebook with five points written down. That was it, her entire teaching plan. Amy believed that if you knew your content, you didn't need a five-page outline to teach a class. And she believed the work of learning was shared equally by everyone in the classroom, as was the work of teaching. "We are all teachers," she said. "I'm just the facilitator."

When Amy was in a room—a classroom or conference room or anywhere else—she used the whole space, not just the front—she didn't believe teachers should be up front and students in back—and she used her body, gesturing largely, in a way that captivated students; they couldn't resist watching and listening to her.

"It was like she was dancing while teaching," Carrie said.

She always had snacks or candy on hand--even wine. She cursed a lot in class, too, and apologized for it, but it was part of her style. And she always went over time by a half hour or an hour—but she didn't apologize for that. Carrie learned to appreciate her generosity. Amy would say, "You can leave, but I have more to say," and most people stayed. She spoke from her heart, and always said that if she couldn't, then she wasn't equipped to teach.

Time and again, people who Amy coached referred to her generous spirit. Carrie would ask to sit down with her briefly, and Amy would block off a half-day, noon to four, just to give her advice.

"Edgewood could not hold her brilliance," said Carrie. "Her voice is still in my head and my heart."

Mustapha Drammeh was another a student of Amy's who holds a special place for her in his heart. Mustapha was working on his MBA at Edgewood when he took Amy's eight-week organizational behavior class.

"She was very direct, always said it like it was, and she was very knowledgeable about her material," he said. "She engaged students and challenged us, encouraged everyone to participate, even if they didn't want to. And she was so flexible and funny. She loved what she was doing, and her passion was contagious, and she was very easy to approach."

Amy's class, recalled Mustapha, was less like traditional classes and more like a feedback session, where students had to do research related to real life and were encouraged to discuss their feelings alongside their thoughts.

"Her class was about sharing from your own experience," he said. "She offered advice about how to stand out, how to empower yourself, and how to look around and think of others."

Mustapha learned something else from Amy: in a class discussion, she pointed out to him that he was complaining about his work a lot, specifically about being stifled by colleagues or superiors when he brought them good ideas. She guided him to understanding how to look around himself and consider how other people are thinking and feeling.

"I want to grow with a project, but there's a guy who's been there ten years longer than I have, and maybe he worries I'll move ahead of him. Amy taught me to think of him."

Annette Miller was a student at Edgewood in 2016, and the class she took with Amy changed her life.

"Amy was invested in and passionate about changing the design of entrepreneurship," said Annette. "And, specifically, she was passionate about how to ensure when we lift women, we also see how we can lift

Black, Indigenous, and other racial ethnic groups of women, too. She did not want women getting caught in male-dominated and centered-mindset thinking, particularly since that design held women back and counted them out for success."

"I fell in love with her on day one," said Annette.

Amy always knew what she wanted to discuss and wasted no time, although her meeting style included a lot of laughing and joking. She was self-deprecating and shared gems from her personal life, herself, and her family with her students, which they found disarming. She was self-deprecating but never apologetic. She was "always late and always coming in hot," said Annette. The friendship with Amy grew outside of the classroom—they were both women in a male-dominated space, and they shared the same priorities. "We were change agents," said Annette. "I always left our meetings feeling like I got a shot in the arm, and it would hold me until I saw her again."

On vacation in Door County, WI
August 2014

CHAPTER TWENTY-EIGHT

• • • • • • • • • • • • • •

One of Amy's central messages crossed professional and personal boundaries: if something is important and meaningful, now is the time for it. Do it now. This was true at work and true at home.

"She was clearly committed to centering her family," said Annette, "and always gave Mike credit for getting the family together to spend quality time. He was the rock, and because her childhood had been unsteady, she appreciated him. His consistency meant everything to Amy, even if sometimes it drove her a little crazy as well. But she stressed a lot about not having enough quality time with the kids."

Mike was also alert to the need for more quality time at home. Between the demands of his work and Amy's, trips were one of the few ways the family could just relax together. He did a little work on the trip to Norway, sure, and had to finish something on the way to Hawaii, but for the most part the family's travels were all play.

With Annette, Amy opened up a few times about her relationship with you, specifically. She worried that she and Jocelyn didn't connect readily enough, but she felt that you got her, which meant that you accepted her as she was and weren't critical that she wasn't living up to expectations.

"She appreciated that Aaron was more chill and laid back about things, and she got more out of their conversations because he was more forthcoming," said Annette.

It's hard to say why some friends knew more about Amy's anxieties than others, or how and when she chose to share, but Annette recalled a side to Amy that not many people saw: There were times when Amy questioned her own parenting skills, those skills that everyone around her recognized and praised. Maybe the early years were easier for Amy, and as her kids grew, she felt more pressure on her parenting. She conveyed to Annette that although there was so much love between herself and her daughter, she was on edge about her relationship with Jocelyn, possibly because she had high expectations given her relationship with her own mother, and sometimes felt she was falling short.

"She was aware of herself," said Annette. "She talked about her parenting and what she wanted. She also saw herself in Jocelyn and Aaron and laughed at how she 'showed up' in their personalities. She felt blessed, and she knew they weren't perfect, but they were family and in it together."

Every so often, the two women argued—mostly about issues relating to race and class. Amy had always leaned into her experience with diverse populations and was proud of her work centering Black women.

"Our sticky issues came up when she believed she understood more than she did. Compared to other white women, Amy could navigate—and sometimes she thought she'd gotten all the way there. We would both react like, 'I don't like what you just said,' and then we'd take a break and come back to each other later. We both needed to process."

That said, Annette recognized something in Amy that other white women don't have. "Women of color loved Amy because she saw them to their core. In Madison, with all the whiteness, well-meaning, and disrespect, she stood out because she did not do that. She listened, supported, and believed, and she helped people believe in themselves," said Annette.

Annette and Amy both spent a lot of time working, and whenever Annette experienced a crisis of confidence, it was Amy who reminded her who she was and what she could do.

"She would say, 'Tits out! Girl, you can do this!'" said Annette. "Those activator statements encouraged me to leave a great job where I could have retired and do my own thing."

With Amy's wind in her sails, Annette left the private sector to start EQT By Design, a consultancy that helps businesses reach diverse communities.

"When I left, I called her, saying 'What did I do?' She said, 'What you were supposed to do. Eyes up.' She made me feel like a badass. As I flew and spread my wings, moments in the past where I had doubted myself, when I had stood up for myself to men in particular, came back to me, and those men ended up apologizing to me. That was a new one. Amy gave me that strength. I never thought I'd see the day when I could express myself and when people would listen, respect, and acknowledge the whole of me."

What did badass mean to Amy?

"It means you have a vision, but you're also scared," said Annette.

Amy gave Annette the key to open herself up and set herself free—to lean into what she knew and be fearless and deliberate in asking for what she wanted while recognizing how to work smart, not hard. She leaned hard on the prioritization analogy about the jar of rocks, pebbles, and sand: The rocks are the most important things in life, like family and health and friends; the pebbles are the other big things, like work and school; and the sand is the small stuff, like material possessions. The jar represents your time. If you fill the jar with big rocks first, then pebbles, then sand, you can make it all fit; but if you put in the sand first, there will be no room for the rocks or the pebbles. Prioritize the big stuff, Amy said, by spending quality time with the people you love—the rest will always find space.

"Amy taught me that if you're going to do social justice work, you need to be smart about your capacity and about what you're going to need to grow and leverage. She believed in going big. She had the characteristics of a leader in a patriarchal world, even though she was centering women. That resonated with people."

But she wasn't perfect and always made that abundantly clear.

"She was perfectly imperfect. That was our catchphrase. It came out all the time, she said it out loud to everyone. But she was a pioneer.

In Madison and at our age, it wasn't common to be around someone so irreverent. And she was irreverent. And intellectually sharp and financially sharp. You couldn't minimize her. And she had really fucking good ideas."

With her mentoring work, and later with the Social Good Accelerator and Doyenne, Amy "helped endorse the legitimacy of the ideas of historically marginalized people and women and helped them fly, pop, and grow!" as Annette put it.

"She had this ability to reach in and pull out the greatness inside a person who isn't accustomed to wearing it on her sleeve. Her use of language was colorful, in all different ways, and she really centered talent and didn't try to make people into something they weren't. She didn't believe women needed fixing—she believed in the power of women and their ideas. That's something I so miss about having her in the world. That gift is rare," said Annette. "She helped people see their own beauty and helped them see what they couldn't."

When Amy had to travel for Aaron's birthday, she made this sign and asked people all over Vancouver to hold it and take a photo that was sent to Aaron
August 2015

CHAPTER TWENTY-NINE

• • • • • • • • • • • • • •

After eight years in the classroom and two years as Interim Dean of the College of Business. Amy's mentoring of entrepreneurs while at Edgewood might have been the first step to making the choice to leave academia behind, It was a move than came after much frustration with Edgewood's patriarchal culture and after much discussion with Mike, who by and large supported the decision despite its fifty-percent pay cut.

"Mike supported her happiness," said Annette about Amy's decision. "She'd done as much as she could at Edgewood and had strong, bittersweet feelings about the place. She'd found her voice there, and now she was liberated to leave because she knew she deserved more." Plus, the connections Amy had fostered gave her a sense of empowerment and confidence she hadn't had before. "She was getting a lot of positive stroking from different corners and spaces, not just inside the institution," said Annette. "This buoyed her even more."

She was in a new phase of life by this time, too. In her late forties, with both kids out of elementary school, she was struggling with hot flashes and mood shifts—and, as Annette put it, she'd entered a phase of life when people jettison the parts of their lives that aren't working for them.

"You're in the next level of life," she said. "Amy was growing into herself in a new way, and she was unapologetic and real about it."

Annette loved Amy's potty mouth, her humor, and her deep compassion. She even loved her impatience and desire for the wheels of social justice to turn more sharply and quickly.

"It's not enough to say she was a coach or a mentor—Amy was inspiring. She helped you see yourself. She got a lot of vitamins from it, but it wasn't about her—she centered you. She built you up to make you strong so you could see what she saw. She was scaffolding."

Amy and Heather Wentler originally met not through business, but through you and Jocelyn. Heather ran a math and science enrichment program called Fractal, which you and Jocelyn attended; after you aged out of the program, Jocelyn and her girlfriends continued privately. The two women spent time with you at the Shorewood pool, too, and Heather saw first-hand how invested Amy was in her family.

"She lived for those kids," said Heather. "She used to say that what she wanted most was for her kids to wake up and feel loved."

Amy's favorite part of the day was driving you both around—Uber-mom, she called it—because that's when she got a glimpse of you both in your natural state, with your friends, in contrast to family dinner, which was often full of forced conversation. She told Heather about the twenty-minute conversations she would have with you about big stuff—consent, drugs, responsibility—where she would sit you down and talk to you like an adult, and then it was over.

"She was a very confident parent," said Heather.

The two women also found themselves in the same room at a start-up event, and they looked around and asked themselves, then each other: Where are all the women?

"We 'dated' a good while before we decided to move forward," said Heather, to make sure it was a good fit. Amy's commitment to Edgewood was fraying—by 2017, when she left, the situation there was ugly, in Heather's words—but it was a lot to give up, the steady pay, benefits, and title. There was a lot of overlap in what the two women wanted to accomplish for marginalized entrepreneurs—they shared the same dream—but they were very different people when it came to the nuts and bolts. When they started Doyenne, and the organization was still small, they gained a lot of traction right away—then the big question was how to grow. Amy had her sights set on a broader scope, and she tended to believe in spending money to make money, while Heather was more process oriented and took things step by step. Building a business together was an intimate partnership, one that brought out their best and worst.

"I felt I could trust Amy when we started out," said Heather. "Like really trust her, like I trust my husband."

Amy was at her best working with entrepreneurs. She loved to patiently dissect people's ideas and help them think through the big picture; she lived for a big idea. When she and Heather were at their best, during Doyenne's infancy and toddlerhood, Amy was as much Heather's coach as her partner. "She worked on the big picture, then I came in with the steps to get there," said Heather. "We tag-teamed. We always got glowing feedback from the entrepreneurs who came through those early programs. Those first years were seamless."

The trouble started, in Heather's view, when Heather was ready to let go of Amy's hand. She no longer needed Amy to sit in on meetings or offer advice, but Amy wasn't ready to relinquish control. Amy gave everything she had in terms of sweat equity, but she couldn't be there one hundred percent of the time. Slowly, she was adjusting to giving up the reins.

Going all-in on Doyenne was a big change from Amy's work in the classroom or coaching—though Heather was like a younger sister to Amy in some ways, she also matched Amy in her strength of will and belief in Doyenne. Sometimes—often, near the end—the women disagreed.

"Your superpower is also your kryptonite," said Heather. "Amy was a confident woman, but sometimes she overcompensated for insecurities or for not having the answer, and she could be defensive. We called each other out on stuff, and we butted heads a lot, which is not a secret. We approached the work from very different angles. Amy loved the big picture and sometimes had a hard time bringing ideas to fruition. I prefer to see how things are working, then make a move."

Often, the two agreed on the goal but not the process for getting there. "I felt that when we were moving forward, Amy added detours. And she felt we missed out on opportunities because I was too practical," said Heather.

Money. It had been years since Amy had lived in the rat-infested apartment in Atlanta, since she'd shared a car, or worried about paying rent. But without the consistency of her teaching position, money was suddenly an issue again, at work and at home. In a start-up, there's no moving money around, no slush fund. The foundation dollars dried up quickly, grants only went so far—they needed more revenue streams. Amy knew Doyenne had the potential to be big—and she believed she could make it big—but in the meantime, there was a good deal of anxiety about the pay cut she'd taken and the funds they needed to grow.

Speaking in broad strokes, Amy's eye was on the future; Heather's was on the bottom line.

Amy was not one to fuss over details. And Amy's vision for Doyenne was so momentous—so audacious, to borrow the organization's tagline—that she sometimes felt insulted when they didn't command the respect they deserved. At one point, while meeting with a potential partner, Amy walked out when an assistant showed up in place of the real deal. "They wanted nothing to do with us after that," said Heather. Amy rankled a few board members, too, at least partly because of her tendency to use the 'F word' in meetings. If Amy received an email or call that she thought wasn't worth Doyenne's time, she didn't respond. She was concerned primarily with accomplishing the Doyenne vision—she didn't spend a lot of time or energy soothing over anything that was getting in the way.

Annette Miller was privy to the internal dynamics at Doyenne and saw the tension mostly as a result of how different the two women were. They wanted to be good partners to each other, though, and struggled with how to do it. They appreciated each other, but they were frustrated.

Alnisa Algood met Amy through a community start-up event when Doyenne was merely a gleam in Amy's eye—but the friendship developed fast. Alnisa recognized right away that Amy was serious about the work of centering marginalized entrepreneurs. She was outgoing, dynamic, and engaging. She brought people to her and made them comfortable, and she was comfortable in the limelight and a good listener at the same time.

"She was so good at getting people to talk about themselves and participate, getting them comfortable in spaces where women and people of color typically don't have a voice. She struck me as someone who made herself open while also being protective of who she was. When you're a woman in predominantly male spaces—or a women and person of color in white male spaces—you need to be able to engage people who are closed to you."

This was one reason Alnisa and her partner brought Amy in to be the third leg of the Social Good Accelerator—because she was a great moderator and dynamic instructor, but she could also interact with Black and Brown women who they were working to center.

"Not a lot of white people can do that," said Alnisa.

For the two years that Amy worked for the SGA, she did so unpaid—there was a plan in place to pay her as a consultant and curriculum designer in 2020. But she was learning as much as she was teaching. From time to time, said Alnisa, Amy got the language of the work wrong—but she was willing to acknowledge and work on it when she made mistakes of language or thought.

"She had a base level of commitment and compassion, which meant that even though she occasionally made mistakes dealing with cultures and communities that weren't her own, she was determined to improve," said Alnisa.

And Amy was flexible, which the community really valued. She made it known that people could come talk to her if their situations didn't accommodate a deadline. She was the SGA's lead instructor and supported the SGA's core philosophy: when it comes to Black and Brown entrepreneurs, 70% of the roadblocks are external, related to what people think of you versus your own work.

"We're highly focused on the pitch and storytelling," said Alnisa, "and we avoid putting more barriers in front of people before they're ready to hurdle them."

Amber Swenor met Amy in 2015 at a business event, while Amy was still at Edgewood. They connected immediately; they had a lot of similar personality traits. Amy didn't care about rules—she cared about doing what was right, and she had the guts to say what needed to be said. This was Amber's style as well.

"I felt totally safe talking with Amy about anything," said Amber, echoing the sentiments of so many people I talked to. "She was judgment-free. Her gift was teaching people how not to judge themselves." Even if you only had two conversations with Amy, you felt connected to her. You felt seen, comfortable, and safe.

Amber was already mid-stride with her start-up when she met Heather and Amy, and she felt she'd found kindred spirits in these women who also had ideas about non patriarchal business models. "You're enough," was their message, and Amber bought it. A year after they met, in 2016, Amy and Heather invited Amber to speak at one of their events, and while she talked through her list of the top craziest things she learned in her first year as a business owner, Amy sat in back, smiling proudly. "She did that for everyone—she got people to tell their true stories. She was there for you."

All meetings ran long, recalled Amber, because Amy spent the first twenty minutes talking about her kids.

Before the accident, puberty was on the agenda—Amy was fascinated by Jocelyn's mood swings: freaking out and then calming down and being cheerful, then freaking out again. She loved being part of the growth journey. "Even when the kids argued, she seemed like she was fully living through the experience. Behind the veil, she enjoyed all the ins and outs of parenting and never took the experience for granted. She had the wisdom to know that being their parent was a special gift."

Amy had it together, or gave that impression, despite running late or losing her keys or needing coffee or chatting about the kids. She was high energy but never frantic or flustered. Sooner than later, she'd get into what needed to be done, and she was wholly present. She made time for people.

Amber and Amy shared the Dias at a Disrupt Milwaukee event—on stage, they both spoke their minds, but they didn't align with the event's directors, so it felt to Amber like they were rebels together, both on stage but refusing to play their game. "They tried to tell Amy what she could and couldn't say," said Amber. "I was like, 'Good luck with that.'"

Amy hired Amber's heavy metal band play for one of Doyenne's birthday bashes, and Amber was not the only one to recall Amy getting up on stage and rocking out. "I loved her spirit and wanted to be girlfriends with her," said Amber, who mentioned that she wished she had a relationship like what Sagashus's shared with Amy. "I wanted to hang out. I wished she'd call me up on those nights when you just want to vent in your pajamas. But I also knew how wide her network was. When she died, I felt a profound loss—I felt that I lost one of the most important people in my life while also recognizing that she was just as important to a lot of people."

The last time Amber spent time with Amy was briefly in October 2019, when Amber was teaching a class on brand strategy to Doyenne accelerator participants; but more meaningful time was spent on a retreat in September of 2019, three months before she was gone. "There are only a few people in your life who tell you things you remember forever. At that retreat, Amy said, 'Amber, people will follow you wherever you go.' For me, she was one of the three most profoundly impactful people in my life."

Amber has done some thinking about Amy's legacy, not only at Doyenne but in you. "She'd wanted Aaron to be free of judgment of himself and others, I think," she said.

"To not be afraid of tough conversations that help you grow as a person. To not be afraid to examine the things that might make you feel uncomfortable. And to be kind without sacrificing your principles. Being kind can change your life and the lives of everyone around you."

Jillana Peterson met Amy through Doyenne in its toddler years, in 2013, and right away felt that they were kindred spirits.

"Amy is the person in the room who runs over to you to introduce herself," she said.

Jillana was never formally a mentee or member of Doyenne—she is not, in fact, an entrepreneur; she works at ZenDesk—and still Amy had an enormous impact on her. Amy made the case the Jillana would be an asset to Doyenne's events committee, and she joined up.

"I can't even describe how much Amy did for me," said Jillana. "She built in me the confidence I have now. Amy pulled me into her world, and I made so many friends who I never would have known."

Amy, said Jillana, slept and breathed empowering women. It was never just work; it was a lifestyle. Together, Jillian and Amy attended a conference in Green Bay, and they stayed in an Airbnb and basically had a slumber party, drinking wine and talking about raising kids. They enjoyed just being together. "Jocelyn was into Lizzo at the time, and Amy and I drove around in her black SUV with the windows down, singing Lizzo songs at the top of our lungs. She was so joyful. I just loved her so much."

Children should be treated like capable humans, Amy told Jillana. They talked about how to talk to boys about pornography, how to let them have phones and navigate social media, and how deeply inspired Amy was by her kids.

In 2017 through 2019, Emma Lucas worked for Doyenne first as a marketing intern in event planning during the last years of Amy's life. In April of 2019 and for the last birthday bash Amy attended, Emma hired four female comedians but didn't vet them beforehand.

"Doyenne clientele is progressive, but the acts were raunchy, and some people were laughing nervously while some people were clutching their pearls. Some people walked out. Afterwards, Amy got up on stage, raised her hands, and said, 'I'm uncomfortable!'" said Emma, who felt responsible. But Amy was supportive of the comics and of Emma.

"She was unapologetic," said Emma, about that night and Amy in general. "She was so honest. She always acknowledged when she was frustrated or angry, which allowed her to share the good and the bad. It made people feel safe. It helped you not be afraid to take risks."

Amy talked to Emma a bit about her kids, specifically about a project Jocelyn was working on about sustainability and food trucks, hoping to influence them to use sustainable cutlery. "Amy said Jocelyn was frustrated because she wanted the whole enchilada—a mile, not an inch. You could tell she was headstrong, cut from the same cloth as her mom." She was figuring out an internship for you at the Spark building, too, and she talked about curling up with you on the sofa and watching shows together.

It was in working with Amy and observing her efforts to develop women that Emma became a braver leader and person.

"Because of Amy, I know when I'm walking into the boys' club, how to stand tall, how to recognize when women are keeping themselves small, and what to do about it."

Mikayla Mitchell started as an intern with Doyenne in 2017, after a disarming interview with Amy during which Amy's casual vibe and friendly encouragement wowed Mikayla on the spot.

"I was Amy's sidekick," she said. "I was never put in a box and never told to stick with what I knew. I offered my own ideas, and they let me run with them."

When Mikayla confessed she was having a hard time with her mother, Amy offered advice, which consisted mainly of reminding her that mothers can be unkind. Mikayla weighed in on applicants and noted that Amy was very good at delivering difficult messages.

"She never just said no, she sent a personal note letting people know what they could do to strengthen their position and apply later on," she said.

Doyenne was a playground for the interns, where they could pursue anything that interested them. Mikayla and Amy worked together on the website copy, which Amy wrote in her signature lengthy prose style and Mikayla wanted to scale down. "It was a lot of words," she said. She wanted to put numbers in graphics instead of sentences and paragraphs, but Amy wanted people to get the feel of Doyenne and not leave with questions.

"She was really attached to her words," said Mikayla kindly. "I encouraged her to summarize."

Mikayla experienced some frustration at Doyenne, which stemmed mostly from her and Amy's different work styles. While Mikayla wanted their effort to be grounded in data and facts, Amy was more driven by ideas and experiences.

"She'd say, let's do twelve user tests, and I'd say, let's be smart about who we choose and how we space things," she said.

Sometimes Mikayla felt like she was spinning her wheels, putting effort toward projects that would never come to completion or chasing ideas. She revered Amy and Heather and looked to place herself in their personalities—and she saw the holes in the partnership and how they could hurt each other without meaning to. Over time, Mikayla relied more on Amy for pep talks than practical advice. Amy taught her not to rush things with men and not to apologize—she said women apologize too much in the workplace and in relationships—and to be confident in her viewpoint.

I never met Amy, but I know many people who knew her at least a little, including Alyssa Kenney, who participated in the Social Good Accelerator through her work with DaneNet, a digital equity initiative.

"I adored Amy," said Alyssa. "She was straightforward, down-to-earth, and could deliver criticism authentically and in a caring way better than anyone I've ever met. I've never received as valuable feedback about the way I speak and present a proposal as I received from her."

Amy would say: What does a layperson need to understand your idea? What's sticky about it?

"It's hard for white women to be authentic around racial equity issues, and she did it well," said Alyssa, who is white. "She was always willing to talk about race in a vulnerable way. She found the words without being condescending or savior-y."

You belonged to a special club if you worked with Amy, and you knew it. Amy's name gave your project validity and power, and you felt like you were part of something bigger.

"When she spoke, I always thought, I wish I'd said that! You said it perfectly! I felt it, and you put it into words," said Alyssa.

Teaching was one of Amy's strengths. She loved it too.
July 2017

CHAPTER THIRTY

• • • • • • • • • • • • • •

Heather and Amy were in a tense place when the family left for Hawaii. They had more than a few angry and emotional conflicts over the past two years—Heather felt the wrath of Amy's temper in a way few people did—and were at an impasse. "She popped into the office to say goodbye, and that was it. We didn't text while she was gone," said Heather.

The relationship and the partnership—one and the same—felt to both women like it was falling apart. They were working with a Human Resources therapist and trying to figure out how to communicate better, but they weren't seeing progress. Together, the partners worked through a ton of strength finders and personality tests. Showering people with gifts was Amy's love language; Heather's was quality time and acts of service. Still, at the time of the accident, Amy was looking into launching a side hustle, consultant work, and she and Mike were communicating more about her reduced paycheck than the value or substance of Doyenne's mission. The field was fogged over with worries about revenue and income.

"She was tired, too," said Heather. "We both were. Ninety percent of the time it was amazing, but then there was the other ten percent. I recently looked at pictures, and I think she was in a period of reformation. The kids were older now, and things had changed. We both aged ten years between 2017 and 2019. For me, it was worth it—but I'm still alive. I don't know how Amy would feel. Was that how she would have wanted to spend the last two years of her life? I'm not sure."

Heather has no plans to replace Amy in Doyenne; she's not emotionally ready to do that and won't be for a while. "I'm keeping her alive in the organization," said Heather. "What comes next will have Amy's influence, but it won't have the benefit of her unique touch."

Carrie Sanders put it this way: "Doyenne is just not Amy, which is a testament to her in itself."

Amy would want Doyenne and the work they do to stand on its own and wouldn't want anything to get in the way of the good they're doing, including her own death.

Amy talked as much with her hands as her mouth.
July 2017

CHAPTER THIRTY-ONE

• • • • • • • • • • • • • •

Chris and Shayna Wright and their daughter Izzy, who was Jocelyn's age, met Amy for the first time outside Dairy Queen. As Shayna tells it, they were minding their own business when some crazy lady they'd never laid eyes on started talking to Izzy, who was just about four years old at the time. As it turned out, Amy recognized Izzy from Jocelyn's preschool. After that, the girls were inseparable. The Wright family had moved to Madison around the same time you did and were still getting acclimated. They lived down the street from your first house on Chamberlain. For the next eleven years, the families spent Christmases and vacations together, camped together over Mother's Day, and spent hours by the fire together. "Amy loved having a fire," said Shayna.

Shayna had a modest upbringing, similar to Amy's, and when your family moved to Shorewood, Amy confided in her that the new house was too fancy, and she wasn't sure she would be happy there. (She was!) Shayna hadn't moved into the world of social justice or diversity, and it was Amy who opened her eyes.

"Amy could really woke a person," she said. "She was my Jedi. She always helped me see things from a different perspective."

Chris felt the same way.

"I was a first-time, one-time dad, and I struggled," he said, "and Amy always seemed to understand the issues I was having."

Like her friends back in Boston, Shayna and Chris could see right away that Amy was special. She was rigorously honest but always kind, had no ulterior motives of any kind, and she wasn't afraid to show her flaws or her crazy, as Shayna called it.

"There was huge crazy in her," she said. "And I loved being a part of it.

Shayna joined Amy on a trip to Malawi with her Edgewood students and got to know Amy's brother Cary, who also joined the group. That was the only time Shayna saw her wearing her professor hat, as she put it. For the most part, the Amy she knew had no reservations or formality. She was a woman who would pee outside because she didn't think she'd make it home or borrow Shayna's beater of a car and enjoy it as much as her fancier one. While Jocelyn and Izzy were at the gym together, Shayna and Amy hung out nearby, then went back to pick up the kids. Shayna was there as Amy grew frustrated with Edgewood, then downright sick of it.

"The old white guys running the place weren't open to new ideas," said Shayna. "Amy was tired of being mansplained, tired of all the bullshit."

Once Amy left Edgewood and Doyenne was up and going, Shayna and Amy spent time playing—drinking, yes, but also just laughing and telling stories. "We were like kids again," said Shayna. Once, they met out at a bar and closed it down, and Amy slept over to avoid driving. In the morning, they found that Amy's car had been towed. "We can't tell Mike!" Amy said to Shayna.

With Amy and Jocelyn gone, Izzy had lost her best friend—and she'd lost Amy, too, a grownup who had always cajoled her into hugs and treated her like a second daughter. "She was always doing fun stuff, getting manicures, taking us to Rockin' Jump or out for pizza," said Izzy. "She was never self-conscious about acting silly, and she didn't treat kids differently. She treated us like people."

Shayna described her own parenting style as reactive and emotional, whereas Amy's was rational and calm.

"She was a disciplinarian but always level-headed. She didn't yell—she thought about it, and then she came up with life lessons," she said.

Amy gave her own kids a lot of responsibility, unlike many parents of her hovering generation, and she stuck to her guns. If it was time to leave for day camp and the kids hadn't packed their own lunch and snack, she'd leave anyway. "Guess you'll be hungry, and next time you'll remember," she said.

Amy was a do-it-yourselfer before it was trendy. She got things done and expected her kids, especially now that they were in school, to be the same way. "If your kid can do something," she said, "then they should do it." This applied to anything from tying their own shoes to putting away dishes. "It doesn't help to take that development away from them," she said.

Shayna saw the way Amy treated their girls—as a champion and a feminist, empowering them and showing them what they could accomplish. Though both girls were gymnasts, Izzy didn't invest herself in the competition the way Jocelyn did. Jocelyn wanted to be the best.

"That was Amy coming through," said Shayna. "She had a competitive drive and desire to make an impact. And she did. She left a big mark."

Like her mother, Jocelyn was already a planner by age thirteen. She researched universities and determined that she was going to earn a gymnastics scholarship to attend Ohio State.

"She was a serious kid, but she could also be goofy, like Amy," said Shayna. "One difference was that Amy had a warmth to her—she was warm to everyone—that maybe Jocelyn would have developed as a grownup."

Very few people I talked to knew that Amy had a temper, but Shayna was one of them. "You would not want to cross her. You might not survive it," she said. Once, they were downtown on the Square, and a young homeless guy started pushing Shayna to hand over some cash. Shayna wasn't comfortable being confrontational, but Amy swooped in. "She got right up in they guy's face and told him to go away," said Shayna. "You don't mess with mama bear."

Once, Shayna introduced Amy to her sister Wendy, and the three women went out together. "I'd never make that mistake again," said Shayna. Where Amy was progressive, emotional, passionate, and wanted to save the world, Wendy was analytical and cool, and eventually, the two started bickering about everything under the sun. They were not fast friends.

"If you didn't like Amy, there was something wrong with you," said Chris about that night.

Shayna brought out the wild in Amy. One summer, the two families shared a nanny named Monica. Before Monica left to go back to college, Shayna and Amy drove her to the Tornado Room in Shayna's MINI convertible. "Amy tied a scarf around her hair like a babushka. We didn't know exactly where Monica lived, so we drove up and down frat row hollering her name. Monica probably thought we were nuts, but to me that night was everything I loved about Amy," said Shayna.

"I was so lucky to have her in my life."

Our last family photo the day before the accident
December 2019

CHAPTER THIRTY-TWO

• • • • • • • • • • • • • •

Amy and Sagashus Levingston met in the fall of 2015, when Sagashus was building her Infamous Mothers brand and seeking entrepreneurial coaching through Doyenne. They became close within a year of knowing each other.

"Amy was all-in on my journey and showed up for me as my coach. We met every week or so, and she was an integral part of what I was able to accomplish," said Sagashus.

Sagashus was a single mom with six kids and a Ph.D. student at the time, sneaking off to start her business while wrapping up her dissertation. "An outsider," she called herself. She'd been raised in a family with traditional values, especially around religion and marriage, and felt there was something powerful in embracing a different path—an infamous path. She and Amy shared a passion for working with issues around race and equity. Doyenne was in its infancy at the time, growing roots in Madison just as Sagashus was putting down her own.

"We were rookies together," said Sagashus, "a new coach and a new player. I was going in a direction that wasn't heard of, and Amy got it. We were co-conspirators."

Amy helped Sagashus through the process of writing her book, building the brand, and launching some programming. She helped with the process of figuring out what Infamous Mothers is all about: turning your infamy into your superpower and taking care of your own health and wellness while you do it. "It's important that women don't collapse at the finish line," said Sagashus. "We help women build a life rooted in freedom."

When they met, Sagashus hadn't yet grown into the brand her business would eventually project; she still felt some shame around her own lack of "respectability," according to the values she'd been taught.

"I was apologetic," she said. "I was hiding."

But there was no hiding with Amy, no shame. The two women forged a friendship from mutual disobedience.

"Amy was a rebel herself. She loved that my work was about rebellion, about empowering women. She taught me that empowerment comes from owning our full selves. Don't amputate parts of yourself to fit in boxes, she said. What she was doing with her company was the same thing I was doing with my brand."

From Amy, Sagashus learned that it can be tricky to coach someone while going through similar stages of business. "Sometimes there was a conflict of interest, so there were periods when we focused more on the friendship and less on the business stuff," she said.

And on top of it all, Amy was a delight. Sagashus loved and appreciated so much about Amy: her short, curly hair and big smile, her friendliness and warmth, her bounciness, bubbliness, and energy. "I could see in Amy that she was in it for the long haul, and that she wanted to be a part of my thing," said Sagashus. She'd jumped from mentor to mentor before meeting Amy—they didn't know what to do with her—but with Amy, she'd struck gold.

"Amy caught me off guard," said Sagashus about those early days. "She was so different from most people—especially people in business. I loved her differences, because they're my differences too. I'm chatty and silly, like Amy was, and I felt that I'd run into a kindred spirit. She felt the same way."

Something they did not share was Amy's love of travel. Sagashus has no interest in travel, and of course Amy loved it, so they developed a tradition where Amy sent Sagashus photographs of places she visited so Sagashus could travel without going anywhere. "I'm a loner," said Sagashus, "I stay home, and I work. I have no interest in going places. But I'm an intellectual, too, so I wanted to hear the history and her opinions on what she saw—without having to deal with the travel part."

Sagashus was one of Amy's few confidantes, too; she was a good listener and supportive. Amy talked to her about the challenges that arose in her marriage and about how important the marriage was to her. She'd talk about how she sometimes felt that although they loved each other and had a great life together, he didn't always understand her work or her passion for it. He was a good man, Amy knew, and though they'd had some rough moments and Mike could be distant emotionally, she believed there were adjustments she needed to make, too, and was committed to making them.

"The men of this world are so messed up," Amy said to Sagashus. "Why would I trade in a good one?"

In 2019, after Amy and Mike returned from a trip to Austin to watch car racing together, Amy was almost giddy with a renewed sense of connection with Mike. "They'd had a breakthrough she was happy about," said Sagashus.

Heather Wentler, too, spoke about Amy's refreshed faith in her marriage after that trip. "I feel like Mike and I really can grow old together," Amy said to her. It might seem like a statement that could be left implied—they were married, after all, and growing old together is part of the package—but in reality, after so many years together, Amy's renewed excitement for the marriage was somewhat radical. Not all marriages last as long as theirs did, and many that do aren't happy. Only the strongest marriages enter the empty nesting stage, which was already on the horizon for Amy and Mike, better off than they started out. Many marriages don't evolve the way it seemed Amy's and Mike's did, especially given all the stressors. It's likely that the evolution Amy was experiencing professionally paralleled the one at home, wherein she and Mike were leaning again into the trust, friendship, and deep love that brought them together twenty-seven years earlier.

Think of ways to be kind and loving to your husband, Amy wrote in a note to herself just before the family left for Hawaii. Maybe this was one of her many ways of growing in middle age—how to love someone better even after loving him for so long.

Amy was a serious feminist, hated man buns, and was a very loyal friend. "If you're mad at someone, she's mad at them," said Sagashus. She hated the month of April and regarded it as a necessary evil to get through (even though both Sagashus's and Jocelyn's birthdays are in April). She was forty-seven and struggling with menopause. "Sometimes she didn't recognize herself," said Sagashus. She felt that her work was not appreciated or recognized in Madison as it should have been—this was one reason that she was invested in growing Doyenne nationally.

She was tremendously proud of her children. She took pride in Jocelyn's spirit and your business savvy and social consciousness. "Being white and male were working against her goals for Aaron," said Sagashus. "She took every opportunity to remind him to be aware of his power and privilege and to consider how he might alleviate oppression for others. He was a teenager, doing teenage stuff, but she held him accountable. She didn't want him to grow up to be a little shit when it came to women."

She was busy, busy, busy. She didn't exercise—she and Sagashus talked about going to kickboxing class together, to vent their frustrations, but they didn't get around to it—but she walked the dogs a lot. They lived in a tony part of town, the kind of neighborhood where everyone knows each other and every other house is undergoing expensive renovations—but that was not her scene. She said she could have just as easily lived in an apartment. And the Gannon house, lovely as it was, was often in at least some form of disarray—but Amy refused to worry about it.

"It's not important to have a clean house—that is not the measure of my life," she said.

She loved going to the movies. She loved the "Wonder Woman" movie that came out in 2019, and she liked "Moonlight," which was hard for Sagashus to sit through. But Amy sat through it because she was trying to be part of a changing ecosystem, one where white people didn't value comfort over knowledge.

Amy loved to eat. "When we had dinner, you'd think my food was for her, and her food was for me," said Sagashus, referring to Amy's tendency to order several dishes at one meal. "She loved variety, so she'd order a couple of main dishes and a couple of sides. When we went for Thai, she always got noodles and soup"—tom yum soup and pad thai—"and she ate meat but usually ordered tofu." For breakfast out, she ordered potato pancakes with applesauce and strawberries and bananas on the side. She preferred vanilla over chocolate—but like Jocelyn, she liked ice cream and ate most kinds happily. Her favorite dessert was strawberry-rhubarb pie.

She used to visit Sagashus at home and draw on the sidewalk with Sagashus's kids. Amy bought all of them beds so they wouldn't have to share. Sagashus didn't know you or Jocelyn, but she had the idea that you were both a little calmer, not wild and crazy like their mom. "I don't know what to do with polite, well-behaved children. My kids are crazy," she said.

Amy didn't believe in God, but she believed in the universe and a higher power.

"There were two Amys," said Sagashus. "One Amy was easy going and supportive, and the other was the Amy who put herself out there for causes she believed in."

When Sagashus needed her most, when an event she'd engineered was being threatened, Amy leveraged her whiteness and her wealth to resolve the conflict.

"She was always aware of her own status, and she used it to balance or overthrow power dynamics," said Sagashus. (About this event, Mike said that Amy had made a good decision, one that he viewed as an investment—but he would have preferred to be consulted first. This was a snag in their generally cooperative union.)

Sagashus described Amy as a big listener but not a big sharer, but unlike many of her friends, Sagashus knew a lot about Amy's childhood, including the name of the street she grew up on—Hog Road, in Greenville, Ohio.

"She struggled to get out and get to college," said Sagashus. "She fought and worked against the culture of her home life, and she always knew her life was going to be different."

The job in Atlanta—the Rape Crisis Center, and the racism she witnessed and called out there—had made a lasting impact on Amy, said Sagashus. In the last years of her life, she'd found a new level of acceptance of her own mother.

"She described her mom as batshit crazy—but not in a really bad way," said Sagashus. "Maybe Amy got her rebelliousness, independence, and defiance from her. They were both stubborn women who knew what they wanted. She had stopped warring with her mother and accepted her as she was. They checked in from time to time, and Amy was invested in her wellbeing."

In the last year of her life, Amy was under a good bit of stress. "She was trying to get her business where she wanted it to go, which stressed her out," said Sagashus.

Donald Trump's presidency stressed her out; she was far from alone in this. "When Hillary lost, Amy was angry and hurt for days," said Sagashus. "It was a moment of real recognition that America does not value women. That was her takeaway. It was a gut punch."

But despite her busy calendar, Amy was not the type who believed in depriving herself of sleep.

"She was always saying that showing up to work on little sleep was like showing up drunk. She was big on the sleep piece. She was always encouraging women to get their rest. And generally, she was vigilant when it came to her own self care. She took vacations, she turned off her phone, and she held her boundaries."

She pulled Sagashus into the world in a way she might not have done for herself, often going together to community events. "We included each other," said Sagashus. "I'm less likely to go out into the world, and she was more likely to, so often when I was out, it was with her."

Amy believed—and taught Sagashus to believe—that entrepreneurship happens within the context of a life, not instead of it.

"If you're a man, often you can make your business into your whole life because maybe there's a partner at home taking care of the kids—but for many of us, it's both/and. Amy gave me the language to understand that life and work are messy and imbalanced," said Sagashus.

Sagashus was the second Black woman to tell me that she'd never met a white woman who understood her privilege like Amy did. "She always let her BIPOC friends know that she would leverage her power if they needed it, if it could help. She pushed us to understand that we are not alone; people with influence can speak up, and she was one of them."

Don't flail, she said. Don't make decisions out of desperation. Make them from a place of empowerment. Even if you have to walk away from the table, do it anyway.

Amy was a Leo—all of Sagashus's friends are either Leos or Aries—which meant she was proud, not big on vulnerability, and a natural-born leader.

"We balanced each other because I'm OK with being vulnerable," said Sagashus. "I take the risk of exposing myself and my internal world."

Amy loved to sing and dance, despite the fact that she did not have a great voice.

"Being good wasn't the point. The point was to be yourself in front of people," said Sagashus. Together, Amy and Sagashus could laugh about inappropriate things—like ugly babies, for example.

"I'd kick it off, and she'd join in. We laughed about things you're not supposed to laugh about. I instigated, but she'd run with it. We laughed together ... uncontrollably."

ABOUT THE AUTHOR
SUSANNA DANIEL

Susanna Daniel is the author of *Stiltsville,* which won the PEN/Bingham prize for best debut, and Sea Creatures, a Target Book Club Pick. She's the co-founder of the Madison Writers' Studio, www.madisonwriters.com, a hybrid creative writing workshop for writers of fiction and creative nonfiction, and lives in Madison, Wisconsin, with her two sons and two dogs. Her third novel *Battersea Road* is forthcoming.

Printed in the United States
by Baker & Taylor Publisher Services